CARDBOARD LOOM
WEAVING

STACKPOLE BOOKS

Published by Stackpole Books
An imprint of The Rowman & Littlefield Publishing Group, Inc.
4501 Forbes Blvd., Ste. 200
Lanham, MD 20706
www.rowman.com

Distributed by NATIONAL BOOK NETWORK
800-462-6420

DANBORU ORIKI DE OSHARE KOMONO HARU NATSU AKI
FUYU ITSU DEMOTSUKURERU TSUKAERU! (NV80357)
Originally published in Japanese language by NIHON VOGUE Corp.,
English language rights, translation & production by World Book Media, LLC
First Stackpole edition 2019

Photographers: Mayumi Abe, Noriaki Moriya
English Translation: Kyoko Matthews
English Language Editor: Lindsay Fair
Contributing Technical Editor: Lucy Anne Jennings
Interior Book Design: Rachel Lawston, www.lawstondesign.com

We have made every effort to ensure the accuracy and completeness
of these instructions. We cannot, however, be responsible for human
error, typographical mistakes, or variations in individual work.

British Library Cataloguing in Publication Information available

Library of Congress Cataloging-in-Publication Data

Library of Congress Control Number: 2018968029

ISBN: 978-0-8117-3833-0 (paperback)
ISBN: 978-0-8117-6846-7 (e-book)

The paper used in this publication meets the minimum requirements
of American National Standard for Information Sciences—Permanence
of Paper for Printed Library Materials, ANSI/NISO Z39.48-1992.

Printed in China

CARDBOARD LOOM
WEAVING

HARUMI KAGEYAMA

STACKPOLE BOOKS

Guilford, Connecticut

INTRODUCTION

I can't tell you how many times I've heard potential students say that they've always wanted to try weaving but think it looks too difficult or are intimidated by the fancy looms. Every time I hear these words, I think it's such a pity because weaving is actually quite simple and can be done with everyday objects.

In fact, I bet you have everything you need to get started just sitting in your recycling bin right now. You guessed it: all of the looms in this book are made from cardboard! Everyone can get their hands on cardboard for little or no cost and it just takes a bit of effort to transform this overlooked material into a working loom. They may look humble, but cardboard looms are just as functional as store-bought ones.

As you flip through the pages of this book, you may find it hard to believe that all of these projects are made on cardboard looms. From beautiful pillows and seat cushions for your home to artful scarves and cozy hats you'll love to wear, this book includes dozens of projects perfect for weaving beginners.

The more I explored the idea of weaving on cardboard looms, the more amazed I was by the possibilities. My hope is that this book makes weaving accessible to everyone!

HARUMI KAGEYAMA

HAVE SOME EXTRA CARDBOARD LYING AROUND?

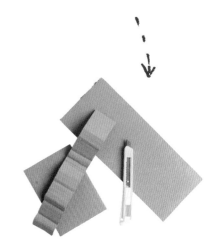

❙ Cut it to size

DON'T TOSS IT! LET'S MAKE A LOOM!

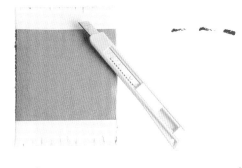

3 Cut some notches

2 Add some tape along the edges

AND NOW YOU HAVE A LOOM!

You can use boxes and flat pieces of cardboard to make different types of looms and weave textiles of all different shapes and sizes.

CONTENTS

LINEN COASTERS

With its small scale and simple design, this project is perfect for weaving beginners. Woven with soft linen yarn, these coasters make a chic addition to any table.

Instructions on page 68

POTHOLDER & TRIVET SET

This set is guaranteed to come in handy in the kitchen! Hemp cord is used for the warp, while torn fabric strips are used for the weft to produce a thick and durable textile. I selected a dark color palette to help camouflage potential stains.

Instructions on page 63

Use the warp yarn to create loops for convenient storage.

In addition to wearing the potholders as oven mitts, you can insert pot handles into the pocket-style openings.

ROUND SEAT CUSHIONS

Brighten up your kitchen
or dining room with these
cheerful fringed seat cushions
woven in the round. These
samples were made from
store-bought t-shirt yarn, but
you can also make your own
from an old t-shirt or piece of
jersey fabric.

Instructions on page 70

SQUARE SEAT CUSHIONS

Both practical and pretty, these colorful seat cushions will keep your skin from sticking to the chair during the hot summer months and keep you warm and cozy during the cooler winter months. Best of all, you can wash them if they get dirty, so no need to worry about messy eaters!

Instructions on page 72

BUTTONED UP PILLOW SHAMS

These simple pillow cases are woven on a three-dimensional box loom, so there's no need for any sewing—just add buttons to keep the pillow form secure inside. Use a soft, thick yarn to add a warm and cozy touch to your living room.

Instructions on page 74

TISSUE BOX COZY

I had a difficult time finding a simple but stylish tissue box cozy, so I designed my own. Try reversing the color placement for a slightly different look.

Instructions on page 76

A button and loop closure allows you to open the cozy and replace the tissue box easily.

STRIPED FLOOR MAT

This classic rug is an excellent way to use up leftover fabric scraps. You can use any colors or prints you desire, but I recommend keeping the fabric weights similar for best results.

Instructions on page 78

AUTUMN
SKY SCARF

Changing the yarn selection
can completely transform the
look of a scarf. This design
uses the same pattern as
the Bouclé Scarf, but has
a lightweight, airy feel.
Use a variegated yarn with
fuzzy pom-poms or slubs to
recreate this look.

Instructions on page 84

BOUCLÉ SCARF

You'll find yourself reaching for this classic scarf again and again—it's the perfect length to wrap around your neck and will keep you warm and cozy on cold winter days. This scarf takes only a few hours to work up, so you can make an assortment in all your favorite colors. Use a fun bouclé yarn for a textured look, as shown here.

Instructions on page 82

RIBBON SCARF

Lengths of colorful ribbon and rickrack are cleverly used as warp threads in this festive scarf design. Experiment with ribbons of different materials, widths, and shapes to suit your personal style. The pale pink yarn provides the perfect backdrop to really make the ribbon pop.

Instructions on page 90

FAUX FUR STOLE

One of the benefits of weaving with fluffy yarn is that you don't have to worry about imperfect stitches. This fancy stole makes an elegant addition to any outfit.

Instructions on page 80

For a different look, position the knot on the side rather than at the center, or try leaving the strings untied.

SCALLOPED SCARF

Warm weather scarves are designed for style over warmth, so you can experiment with the color, shape, and texture to create a truly unique accessory. This lightweight scarf features fuzzy novelty yarn in a vibrant green color scheme and a modern, wavy silhouette.

Instructions on page 86

BLOOMING FLOWERS SCARF

Festive pink pom-poms bloom from a framework of sheer beige yarn in this striking scarf design. Pair with a simple dress or t-shirt to really showcase the beauty of this artful accessory.

Instructions on page 88

SUEDE STRIPED SCARF

Perfect for both men and women, this design features shades of gray and brown wool yarn accented with lengths of suede cord for a chic, high-end look. Match the width of the suede cord to the width of the yarn and weave tightly to produce a warm, luxurious scarf.

Instructions on page 92

COLOR STUDY SCARF

I find it so interesting to watch how the different colors of yarn interact with each other as they're woven together. In this design, four different shades of soft mohair yarn are woven together to create a colorful plaid scarf.

Instructions on page 94

LOOP SCARF

At first glance, this may look like an ordinary scarf, but it includes a special row of buttons, which transforms the design into a cowl. Choose a soft, textured yarn to up the cozy factor even more.

Instructions on page 96

Wrap the scarf around your neck, then insert the buttons through the woven grain to transform into a cozy cowl.

ARTIST'S MUFFLER

This colorful cowl may look like a high-fashion design, but it's actually quite simple to weave tubular pieces when working on a box-shaped loom.

Instructions on page 98

GRASSY MEADOW WRAP

Inspired by a green meadow, this wide scarf features a loose weave and soft, textured yarns. It's the perfect accessory for those breezy spring evenings.

Instructions on page 100

SNOWFLAKE SHAWL

Keeping a monochromatic color palette allows you to experiment more freely with different textures and weights of yarn. This graceful shawl combines loopy novelty yarn and fuzzy mohair for an ethereal look.

Instructions on page 102

FLUFFY WRIST WARMERS

These cozy wrist warmers are ready to wear once they're removed from the loom. They even feature a space for your thumb, allowing your fingers to move freely. This sample uses the same type of yarn as the Faux Fur Stole on page 17, so you can wear the designs together as a coordinating set.

Instructions on page 104

COLORFUL WRIST WARMERS

Made from lightweight cotton yarn, these wrist warmers are useful in spring, or even in the summer if you work in an air-conditioned office. Use a cheerful, bright color palette for added fun.

Instructions on page 106

These versatile leg warmers can also be worn as boot toppers—simply tuck one end into your favorite pair of boots, then fold the top down. Your legs will stay nice and toasty!

LOVELY LEG WARMERS

Weave long, thin tubes to create custom leg warmers. Incorporate contrasting colors and stripes of varying thickness for a modern look.

Instructions on page 108

BUTTON CAP

The beauty of this hat lies in the little felt pom-poms attached to the very tips—the pom-poms can be fastened to create a fitted silhouette or worn free for an entirely different look.

Instructions on page 110

The hat can also be worn unfastened to create this fun cat-eared silhouette.

POM-POM HAT

When weaving, there's no need for complicated decreases as in knitting—just weave a tube and gather one of the ends. Top this classic hat with a big fuzzy pom-pom for a playful look.

Instructions on page 112

TOTE & DRAWSTRING POUCH SET

Believe it or not, these bags are created using the same process as the Pom-Pom Hat on page 29. Notice a subtle difference in color between the tote and drawstring pouch? The warp and weft threads were switched to create a totally different impression.

Instructions on page 114

This handle is created from two separate pieces of ribbon attached at the sides of the bag, allowing you to adjust the length of the strap to suit your preference: shoulder bag or cross-body purse, the choice is yours!

POM-POM SHOULDER BAG

Interesting novelty yarn and wide linen ribbon combine to transform this simple bag into a must-have accessory. The bag even features a lining, making it both beautiful and practical.

Instructions on page 118

The large flap prevents the contents of the clutch from spilling out. The bag is large enough to store a camera or phone.

CONFETTI CLUTCH

This design features a unique construction method in which the flap is woven right on the loom along with the rest of the bag. Torn fabric strips are used for the weft to create a tightly woven, durable bag.

Instructions on page 120

WEAVING BASICS

The process of hand weaving is fairly simple: You always start by stringing the loom with the warp, or vertical threads. Next, you'll pass the weft, or horizontal thread, over and under alternating warp threads. By passing the weft back and forth across the warp, you're weaving a textile!

The warp and weft are the two main components of weaving, unlike knitting, which is done with one continuous thread. Because the warp and weft are separate, you can use different yarns in different combinations to create interesting effects. Let's discuss some of the elements of weaving that can be altered in order to produce unique textiles.

1. YOU CAN USE A DIFFERENT NUMBER OF STRANDS FOR THE WARP AND WEFT.

Fewer strands will create a fine, thinly woven textile, while more strands will create a thicker textile. You can alter the number of strands to produce different effects.

For example, you can use more strands for the weft in order to produce a thicker textile without adding volume to the fringe. Conversely, you can use more strands for the warp in order to make the fringe more voluminous.

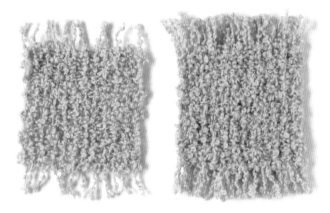

1 warp strand
2 weft strands

3 warp strand
2 weft strands

2. YOU CAN USE DIFFERENT TYPES OF YARN FOR THE WARP AND WEFT.

Simply changing the type or color of the yarn used will have a dramatic effect on the finished appearance of the textile. Don't be afraid to use yarns that are completely different within the same piece.

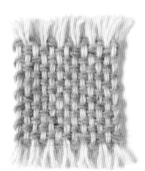

You can use the same type of yarn in different colors—this will create a checkered pattern!

You can use two yarns with different thicknesses.

You can combine many different types of yarn within the same piece.

3. YOU CAN CONTROL THE TIGHTNESS OF THE WEAVE.

Leaving a small gap between the weft rows will produce a loosely woven textile, while leaving no space between the rows will produce a tightly woven textile. Consider the end use when determining the weave—you'll probably want a tightly woven fabric for a functional object like a bag, or maybe a loosely woven fabric for a lightweight scarf.

You can even vary the density of the weave within the same textile.

4. YOU CAN USE UNIQUE MATERIALS FOR WEAVING.

Don't limit yourself to yarn—you can cut old t-shirts, sheets, or fabric scraps into strips for weaving. You may be surprised to discover how different the woven textile looks from the original fabric.

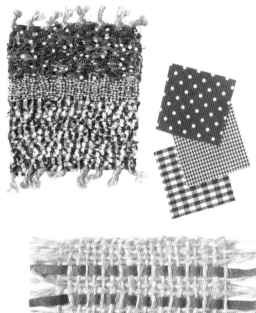

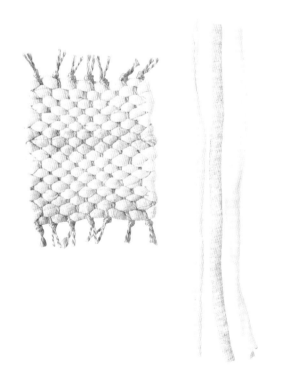

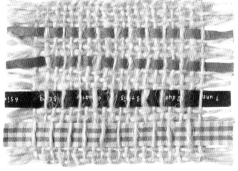

When working on a cardboard loom, you can even use ribbon and leather cord, which are often too wide for store-bought looms. I recommend using these materials as warp threads to add interesting accents within the textile.

ALL ABOUT YARN

Yarn is available in a wide range of weights, from super fine to super bulky. I recommend using bulky or super bulky yarn for cardboard weaving, although lighter yarns are often incorporated into projects for decorative purposes. The following guide features the main types of yarn used for the projects in this book. Use these general properties to help choose the best yarn for your project.

BASIC YARNS

Plied Yarn
This type of yarn is composed of two or more singles yarns twisted together. The twisting process makes the yarn stronger and springier than singles yarns.

Cord
Natural fibers, such as hemp and linen, make strong, durable cord perfect for use as warp thread in projects that will receive a lot of wear and tear, like rugs. Cord also works well as a warp thread when weaving with fabric strips.

Singles Yarn
Singles, or one-ply yarns, are single strands held together by just a bit of twist. Typically, this type of yarn is more delicate than plied yarn. Roving is a type of singles yarn used in this book.

NOVELTY YARNS

The term novelty yarn encompasses a wide variety of yarns made with special effects, such as slubs, loops, and pom-poms, that will produce a textile with a unique texture. Because the yarn itself is irregularly shaped, the woven grain will not always be visible in the finished textile. Let's explore a few of the different types of novelty yarns used in this book.

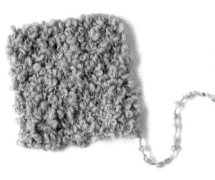

Loop Yarn
Also known as curled yarn, loop yarn is formed by wrapping a textured yarn around a base yarn in a way that small circles or loops protrude from the surface.

Slub Yarn
This type of decorative yarn is created by varying the tightness of the twist at different intervals, which produces a yarn that's thicker in some spots and thinner in others.

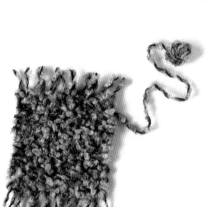

Bouclé Yarn
Bouclé yarn is a type of loop yarn created by loosely looping a textured yarn around a base yarn. This creates an interesting bumpy texture.

Other Novelty Yarns
There are so many different types of novelty yarns that it's impossible to include them all here. Some other novelty yarns used in this book include: ribbon, flag, ladder, and pom-pom. Have fun experimenting with different novelty yarns to add unique texture to your weaving.

WEAVING TOOLS

You'll need a few basic tools to make the looms and weave the projects in this book. Most of these tools are common craft supplies that you may already have on hand.

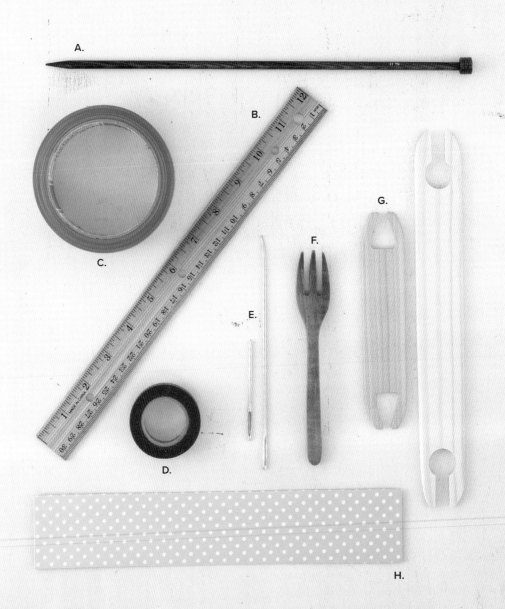

A. KNITTING NEEDLE & B. RULER (SHED STICKS A & B)

A shed stick is a tool that helps you weave the weft thread quickly, without having to manually insert it over and under each warp thread. Use a knitting needle or chopstick as shed stick A to lift one set of warp threads and use a ruler as shed stick B to lift the opposite set of warp threads on the return pass. A ruler is also helpful to measure the width of your woven textile.

C. DUCT TAPE

Duct tape is used to construct the looms in this book. Duct tape works well because it's durable and won't rip during the weaving process. Plus, it won't leave behind adhesive or damage your yarn.

D. MASKING TAPE

Also referred to as washi tape, this thin paper tape is used to secure the end of the warp thread to the loom, and even to secure the loom to the table. The adhesive on this type of tape is not very sticky, so it won't damage your yarn or work surface.

E. NEEDLES

Use needles to weave the weft thread through the warp threads when working on flat looms and box looms. A tapestry needle is also used to finish thread ends, while a long weaving needle is helpful when weaving wide designs.

F. FORK

Use a fork to pack down or adjust the weave as you work. I prefer to use a wooden fork since it won't damage the yarn.

G. SHUTTLES

Weft yarn is wrapped around a shuttle, then passed between the warp threads during weaving, especially when working on table looms. You can buy ready-made shuttles in a variety of lengths, or make your own from cardboard, as shown on page 124.

H. HEADER

Use a strip of cardboard as a guide to mark the beginning and end of weaving on the loom, or to serve as a placeholder for fringe. Cut your header so it is slightly wider than your loom.

ABOUT CARDBOARD LOOMS

You guessed it: You'll need some cardboard in order to make the looms used in this book. You'll also need a few other tools to transform a cardboard box into a loom, but you most likely already have these items lying around. There are a few things to keep in mind when selecting the cardboard to use for your loom.

YES

Close Up

Most of the cardboard boxes commonly used for shipping and storage can be used to make looms. Just make sure that the box is made from corrugated cardboard, which features a ruffled middle layer. If you look closely, you'll see that this type of cardboard has evenly spaced lines on the surface. Look for corrugated cardboard with lines spaced about ⅜ in (1 cm) apart.

NO

Close Up

Avoid double-walled corrugated cardboard boxes, such as the ones used for storing fruit, as this type of cardboard is too firm to use for looms.

SOMETIMES

Corrugated cardboard with lines spaced about ¼ in (5-7 mm) apart is not suitable for general cardboard looms. However, this type of cardboard can be used when weaving with thinner yarn, such as linen cord.

TYPES OF CARDBOARD LOOMS

The looms used in this book are very simple: They are strung with warp, or vertical threads, then the weft, or horizontal thread, is passed through. This repetitive motion is known as weaving. Although they all share the same basic mechanics, there are three different types of cardboard looms which can be used to create woven projects with unique characteristics.

Throughout the book, you'll see these symbols indicating which type of loom is used to construct each project.

TABLE LOOM

A cardboard table loom consists of two flat pieces of cardboard, each with a set of notches at one end. The two pieces of the loom can be positioned on a table for weaving. The distance between the two pieces will determine the length or width of the woven textile. This type of loom allows you to weave larger items, such as scarves, wraps, and rugs.

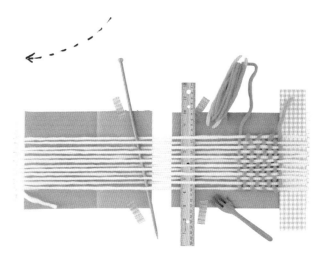

FLAT LOOM

This type of loom features notches for the warp threads at both the top and bottom. It can be used to weave smaller items, such as coasters and placemats.

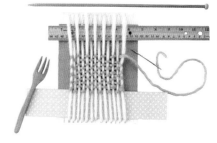

BOX LOOM

Unlike the other looms, which are constructed from flat pieces of cardboard, this loom is a three-dimensional box. Yarn is wrapped around the box to form the warp. The resulting textile will be tube-shaped, which can be used to create neck warmers, bags, and hats.

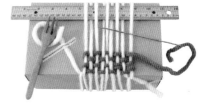

TABLE LOOM

This type of loom is actually composed of two separate pieces, positioned on top of a table. Because you can adjust the position of the pieces, table looms are ideal for weaving large projects, such as scarves and rugs.

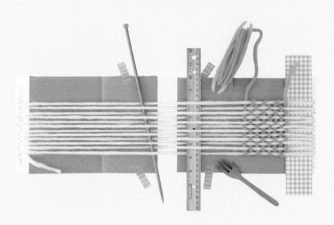

HOW TO MAKE A TABLE LOOM

Tools & Materials

- Cardboard box*
- Duct tape
- Craft glue
- Pencil

- Craft knife
- Ruler
- Masking tape

*The width of the cardboard loom should equal or exceed the desired width of the finished textile, plus ¾ in (2 cm).

1 Cut along the vertical fold lines to separate the box into four pieces (each piece will be composed of the top, side, and bottom portions of the box). You should have two sets of matching pieces.

2 Apply glue to the top portion of one piece. Fold the top down and glue in place so it overlaps with the side portion. Note: If the top portion of your box is larger than the side, trim it to match before gluing in place.

3 Use the palm of your hand to flatten and crush the overlapped cardboard about 1¼ in (3 cm) from the folded edge.

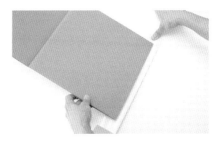  

4 Next, you'll apply duct tape to the folded edge. Cut a piece of tape that is ¾ in (2 cm) longer than the cardboard on each end. Align the folded edge of the cardboard along the center of the tape.

5 Clip into the extending ¾ in (2 cm) areas to meet the cardboard.

6 Fold the clipped tape to cover the left and right edges of the cardboard. Fold the other half of the tape from step 4 down and secure in place.

7 Use the corrugated cardboard lines to determine the notch locations. Mark the notch locations along the tape.

8 Cut ⅝ in (1.5 cm) deep notches along the marked locations.

9 Repeat steps 2-8 to make another piece of the loom.

10 Align one of the loom pieces with the corner of the table, making sure that the notched end is positioned along the edge of the table. Secure the loom in place using masking tape.

11 Each project will state how far apart to position the two pieces of the loom, but at a minimum, the distance from end to end should equal the desired finished length of the textile, plus 2 in (5 cm).

12 Secure the other loom piece in place with masking tape. Double check to make sure that the notches are aligned on the two pieces of the loom.

String the Loom

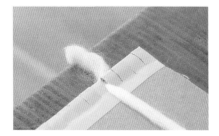

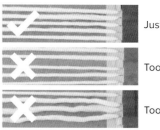

Just right!

Too tight!

Too loose!

1 Leaving a 1 ¼ in (3 cm) long tail, insert the warp thread through one of the notches. It doesn't matter which notch you start with, as long as you'll have enough space to reach the desired textile width. If your project instructions require using two or more strands of yarn, just bundle them together as one when stringing the loom.

2 Bring the thread down to the other loom piece and insert it through the corresponding notch. For example, if you inserted it through the fourth notch in step 1, insert it through the fourth notch here.

3 Continue inserting the thread through corresponding notches. Make sure that the warp threads have the proper tension. If they're too tight, your textile will shrink dramatically when you remove it from the loom. If they're too loose, it will be hard to weave.

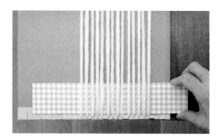

4 String the loom until the warp threads measure ⅜-⅝ in (1-1.5 cm) wider than the desired finished width of the textile. Cut the yarn, leaving a 1 ¼ in (3 cm) long tail.

5 Starting from the right edge of the loom, insert a ruler under and over alternating warp threads. This will be shed stick B.

6 Insert a header under all of the warp threads and position it at the bottom of the loom. If your piece will not have fringe, you can omit this step.

Weave the Weft Thread

7 Next, wrap the weft thread around the shuttle to prepare for weaving.

8 Rotate the ruler so it is standing up straight. This will lift one set of warp threads to create a space, known as the shed. Insert the shuttle through this space from right to left.

9 Leave a 4 in (10 cm) long thread tail, then adjust the weft thread so it is aligned with the header. The first row is complete. If your design does not have fringe, and therefore does not use a header, position the first row right at the end of the notches, as shown on page 47.

10 Starting from the left edge of the loom, insert a knitting needle under and over the opposite warp threads as in step 5. This will be shed stick A.

11 Raise the knitting needle to open the shed and insert the shuttle through from left to right. This will become the second row.

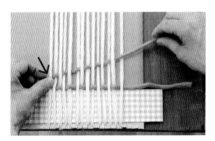

12 Use your thumb to hold the intersection of the warp and weft as you pull the weft down into place. Take care not to pull too hard as this will affect the width of the textile.

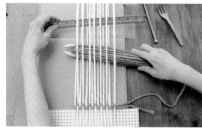

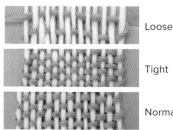

Loose

Tight

Normal

13 Use your fingers or a fork to pack down the weave. Two rows are now complete.

14 Remove the knitting needle. Rotate the ruler and insert the shuttle through from right to left. Repeat steps 10-14 to continue weaving, tightening as you work.

15 You can adjust the tension to create your desired look. For a tight weave, use a fork to pack the rows close together. For a loose weave, leave space between each row.

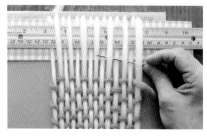

16 It will become difficult to pass the shuttle through as you near the end of the loom. When this happens, lift the top portion of the cardboard loom to create some space between the loom and the warp threads.

17 When you can no longer pass the shuttle through, thread the weft onto a tapestry needle and continue weaving under and over alternating warp threads.

Move the header from the bottom of the loom up to the top and use it as a placeholder to mark the end of weaving/start of fringe (if you are making fringe; otherwise, continue weaving as far as you can). Stop weaving when you reach the header. Remove the header and ruler.

18 To finish the weft thread, weave it through the warp threads between the final and second to last row, passing it under the same warp threads as the second to last row.

19 Once you've woven the weft through half of the warp threads, trim the excess.

20 Use the same process to finish the weft thread tail left at the beginning of weaving in step 9. Refer to page 46 for instructions on finishing the warp threads.

Table Loom Weaving Tips

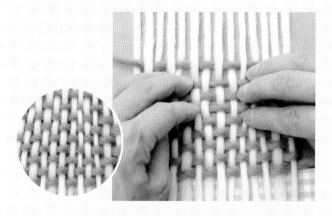

When the Warp is Too Tight

If the warp is too tight, the textile will become too narrow. Use your fingers to spread out the warp threads, making sure that they're straight.

How to Add a Weft Thread

Overlap the beginning of the new weft thread and the end of the old weft thread, then weave together for 2 in (5 cm). Once you've completely finished weaving, trim the excess yarn.

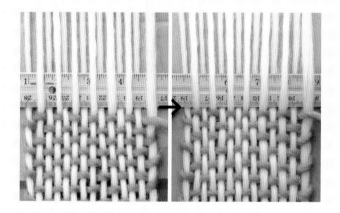

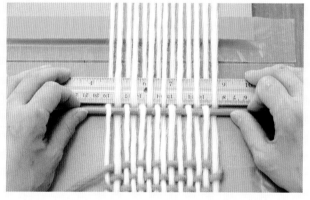

Other Ways to Use a Ruler

In addition to serving as a shed stick, a ruler is also useful for checking and adjusting the width of the textile as you weave. Periodically measure the textile's width and use the ruler to adjust the weft rows.

How to Check The Shed Sticks

To make sure you're using the shed sticks properly, bring the ruler and knitting needle together. If they are threaded correctly, they should alternately pass over and under the same warp threads.

WARP THREAD FINISHING METHODS

There are a few different ways to finish the warp threads. Each option produces a unique look, so choose the method that works best with the design and end use of your project.

Method A Simple Fringe

1 Gently pull to remove the looped warp thread sets from the loom. Lift up the first set. Use a toothpick or skewer to apply fabric glue to the final weft thread in the spot where it is overlapped by the warp thread.

2 Put the warp thread down. Use your finger to secure the warp thread to the glued area of the final weft thread.

3 Repeat steps 1 and 2 until all the overlapping warp threads are glued. Next, flip the textile over. Use the same process to glue the overlapping warp threads on this side of the textile.

4 Once the glue is dry, trim the fringe to the desired length. If necessary, use a ruler to make a straight cut.

A Note on Fabric Glue: When selecting fabric glue, look for one that dries quickly and is washable.

Method B Knotted Fringe

1 Cut the first set of warp threads at the notches to remove them from the loom.

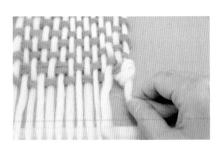

2 Make a single knot using the first two warp threads as a set.

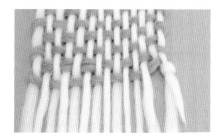

3 Tighten the knot, taking care not to pull the yarn too hard. Repeat steps 1 and 2 to knot the remaining warp threads in sets of two. If you have an odd number of warp threads, use three for one of the sets.

4 Trim the fringe to the desired length.

Method C No Fringe

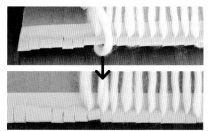

1 Insert the warp thread tail through the second to last notch and twist the tail around the warp thread that was already strung through that notch. Repeat with the warp thread tail from the beginning of the loom.

2 Start weaving the weft thread without leaving any space for fringe. Once you've woven the second row, weave the weft thread tail through the warp threads following the same over and under pattern as the second row.

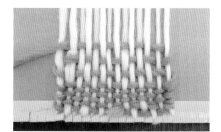

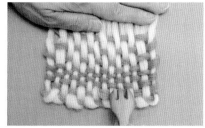

3 Weave the first 3-4 rows tightly. Continue weaving with normal tension, then weave the last 3-4 rows tightly. Weave the weft thread tail in as shown in step 18 on page 44.

4 Remove the textile from the loom. Use a fork to adjust the weave so the tension is even for all rows, spreading out the tightly woven rows to fill the loops where the work was removed from the loom.

FLAT LOOM

This type of loom is very simple: It's composed of a flat piece of cardboard and features notches at both the top and bottom. Flat looms are perfect for weaving small items, such as coasters and placemats.

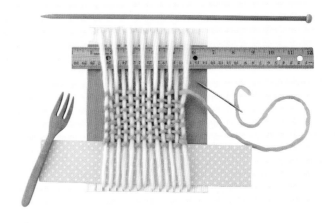

HOW TO MAKE A BASIC FLAT LOOM

Tools & Materials

- Cardboard
- Duct tape
- Pencil
- Craft knife

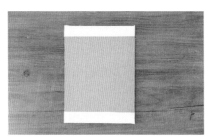

1 Cut a flat piece of cardboard according to the size listed in the project instructions. Position the corrugated cardboard lines vertically. Flatten the top and bottom edges, and apply duct tape, as shown on pages 40-41.

2 Use the corrugated cardboard lines to determine the notch locations. Mark the notch locations along the tape at the top and bottom of the loom. Cut ⅝ in (1.5 cm) deep notches along the marked locations.

HOW TO WEAVE ON A BASIC FLAT LOOM

1 Leaving a 1 ¼ in (3 cm) long tail, insert the warp thread through a notch at the top of the loom. Bring the thread down to the bottom of the loom and insert it through the corresponding notch.

2 Continue inserting the thread through the corresponding notches until the warp threads measure ⅜ -⅝ in (1-1.5 cm) wider than the desired finished width of the textile.

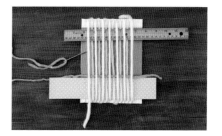

3 Starting from the right edge of the loom, insert a ruler under and over alternating warp threads. This will be shed stick B. Insert a header under all of the warp threads and position it at the bottom of the loom. Rotate the ruler to open the shed. Insert a needle threaded with the weft through this space from right to left, leaving a small thread tail.

4 Starting from the left edge of the loom, weave the threaded needle over and under the opposite warp threads as in step 3. Follow the process used in steps 3 and 4 to weave until the textile reaches the desired length. If it becomes difficult to weave, switch the ruler out for a knitting needle (shed stick A).

5 Weave in the weft thread tails as shown in step 18 on page 44. Refer to page 46 for instructions on finishing the warp threads.

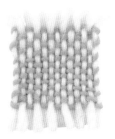

6 The textile is complete.

Note: It may be difficult to use a shuttle for small projects, such as a coaster. Instead, just use a tapestry needle to weave the weft thread.

FLAT LOOM VARIATION FOR ROUND TEXTILES

The unique characteristic of this type of loom is the fact that it has notches positioned on all four sides, which enables you to create a round textile, such as a coaster or potholder. You can also use this type of loom to weave square or rectangular designs—just use the notches along the top and bottom edges, ignoring the ones along the sides.

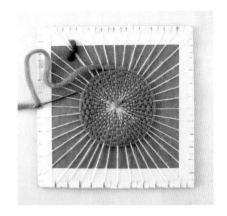

HOW TO MAKE THE LOOM

Tools & Materials

- Cardboard
- Duct tape
- Pencil
- Craft knife

1 Cut the cardboard into a square according to the size listed in your individual project instructions. Flatten the edges, then apply duct tape to all four sides, as shown on pages 40-41.

2 Use a separate piece of corrugated cardboard as a guide to mark the notch placement on all four sides. Cut the notches, as shown on page 48.

HOW TO WEAVE

String the Loom

1 Leaving a 1 ¼ in (3 cm) long tail, insert the warp thread through the second slit from the corner, as noted by ①. Bring the thread across the loom diagonally and insert it through the second slit from the opposite corner, as noted by ②.

2 Next, insert the thread through the second slit along the adjacent side of the loom, as noted by ③. Bring the thread across the loom diagonally and insert it through the second slit from the corner on the remaining side of the loom, as noted by ④.

3 Insert the thread two notches away from ④. Bring the thread across the loom diagonally and insert it two notches away from ③. Repeat this process to continue stringing opposite sides of the loom.

 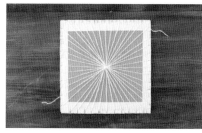 

4 This photo shows what the loom will look like when it's halfway strung. As you work, adjust the thread so the crossed section is positioned at the center of the loom.

5 Use the same process to string the remaining two sides of the loom. Count and make sure you have an even number of warp threads. Cut the excess thread, leaving a 1 ¼ in (3 cm) long tail.

6 You'll need to have an odd number of warp threads to produce a round textile since you are weaving continuously. Simply bind two adjacent warp threads together with a small piece of colorful yarn.

Weave the Weft Thread

  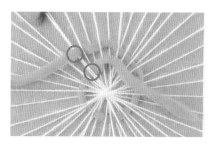

7 Thread a tapestry needle with a 1-2 yd (1-2 m) long piece of weft thread. Starting from the warp threads bound together in step 6, alternately weave the weft thread under and over the warp threads.

8 Once you've made it about ¼ of the way around, pull the weft thread through, leaving a short tail as shown. Continue weaving the weft thread to complete one round.

9 When you begin the next round, the weft thread should pass over the warp threads bound together in step 6, which should be opposite to the previous round. If it's not, you missed a warp thread, so check your work before continuing.

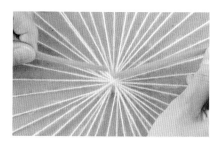 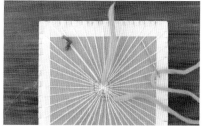 

10 Pull the weft thread at both ends to tighten the first round and bring it to the center of the loom.

11 Follow this process to weave the first few rounds, tightening the weave at the end of each round. After the first few rounds, you'll need to tighten the weave every 6-10 warp threads.

12 It's important to note that the round textile will shrink slightly when you remove it from the loom. Weave an extra round or two larger than your desired finished size to compensate for this shrinkage.

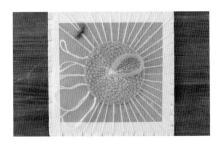

13 To finish the weft thread, weave it through the warp threads between the final and second to last row, passing the weft thread under and over the same warp threads as the second to last row.

14 Once you've woven the weft thread end through five warp threads, trim the excess yarn. Make sure to cut the yarn at an angle so it is not noticeable.

15 Unhook the warp threads from the notches to remove the work from the loom. Knot the warp thread sets at the edge of the round woven textile as you work. Take care not to pull the warp threads too tightly as this may affect the shape of the textile.

Finish the Textile

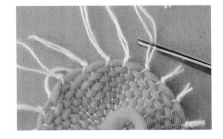

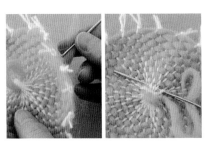

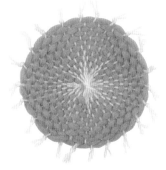

16 Once all the warp threads have been knotted, trim to create the desired fringe length.

17 Thread the beginning weft thread tail from step 8 onto a tapestry needle. Insert the needle through the textile to bring it to the wrong side. Pass under a few warp threads, then trim the excess yarn.

18 The textile is complete!

DOUBLE-SIDED WEAVING

With this technique, you'll wrap the warp yarns around the flat loom, then weave each side to produce a three-dimensional textile, such as a bag. Although this technique uses a flat loom, the warping and weaving methods are very similar to working on a box loom (refer to page 59). This type of loom can be used to create thin bags, such as pouches and card cases.

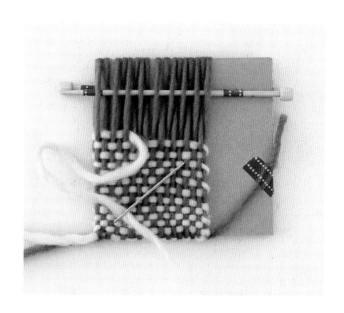

HOW TO MAKE THE LOOM

Tools & Materials

- Cardboard
- Craft knife

Cut the cardboard according to the size listed in your individual project instructions. Flatten the edges with your fingers.

HOW TO WEAVE

String the Loom

1 Starting at the bottom right corner of the loom, wrap the warp thread around the loom. Twist the beginning thread tail around the first warp thread, then tape it to the loom.

2 Flip the loom over and check to make sure the yarn is wrapped in the same way on the back. Twist the end thread tail around the final warp thread along the bottom of the loom.

3 Flip the loom over to the front. Secure the end thread tail to the loom with a binder clip. Starting from the right edge of the loom, insert a knitting needle under and over alternating warp threads.

Weave the Weft Thread

4 Flip the loom over to the back. Starting from the right edge of the loom, insert another knitting needle over and under alternating warp threads. The last warp thread traveled over the knitting needle on the front, so make sure the first warp thread passes under the knitting needle on the back.

5 Flip the loom over to the front. Raise the knitting needle to open the shed. Insert a weaving needle threaded with weft through this space from left to right along the bottom of the loom.

6 The first row is complete. This will be the bottom of the pouch. Starting from the right edge of the loom, insert the weaving needle over and under the opposite warp threads as in step 5.

Back

7 Flip the loom over to the back. Starting from the right edge of the loom, insert the weaving needle under and over alternating warp threads. Two rows are now complete.

Back

8 Starting from the left edge of the loom, insert the weaving needle over and under the opposite warp threads as in step 7. Then, flip the loom over to the front and finish weaving the third row on this side. Follow this process to weave each row on both sides of the loom. After the third row is complete, you can remove the binder clip.

9 A gap tends to form along the edge of the loom where you switch between the front and back. Adjust the stitches to fill the gap as you weave.

10 As you near the end, you may need to remove the knitting needle in order to finish weaving.

11 For the final row, make sure that the weft thread passes under and over the opposite warp threads as the previous rows on both sides of the loom.

12 The textile is complete. Remove it from the loom. You can use either side of the textile as the right side—just choose your favorite, then weave in the thread tails.

DOUBLE-SIDED WEAVING WITH A FLAP

This technique uses the same process as the double-sided weaving technique on page 53, but the weft thread travels around both the left and right edges of the loom. The other benefit of weaving on this type of loom is that you can create a flap, which is perfect for making useful little pouches. Refer to page 123 for instructions on making the loom.

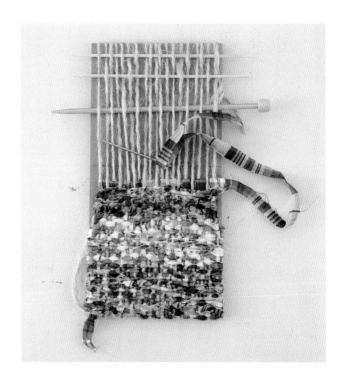

HOW TO WEAVE

String the Loom & Weave the Weft Thread

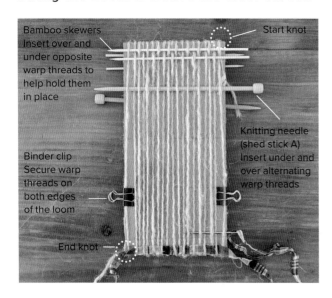

Bamboo skewers
Insert over and under opposite warp threads to help hold them in place

Start knot

Knitting needle (shed stick A) Insert under and over alternating warp threads

Binder clip Secure warp threads on both edges of the loom

End knot

String the loom following the same process used on page 54, but position the start knot along the top edge of the loom and the end knot along the bottom edge of the loom. This will produce an odd number of warp threads. Insert the knitting needles and bamboo skewers through the warp threads on both sides of the loom as shown at left. Starting from the left edge of the loom, insert a weaving needle threaded with weft over and under opposite warp threads from the knitting needle. The first row is complete. This will be the bottom of the pouch.

2 Next, raise the knitting needle to open the shed. Insert the weaving needle through this space from right to left, traveling under and over opposite warp threads as in step 1.

3 Flip the loom over to the back. Repeat step 2 to complete the second row on this side of the loom. Flip the loom over to the front.

4 Repeat steps 2 and 3 to continue weaving, packing down the weave as you work. Stop weaving when you reach the guideline marking the pouch opening.

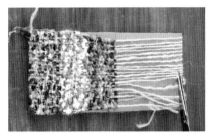

5 Next, you'll continue weaving to make the flap. Make the flap by weaving rows back and forth on the front of the loom only—do not flip the loom over as you work.

6 Stop weaving when you reach the guideline marking the flap end. Finish the weft thread by weaving it in and trimming the excess. Then, cut the warp threads along the top of the loom.

7 Knot the warp threads together in sets of two to make fringe along the flap end. Trim the fringe to the desired length.

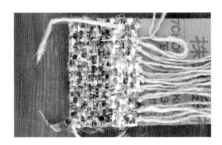

8 Flip the loom over. Knot the warp threads together in sets of two along the pouch opening. Weave the warp threads in and trim the excess.

9 Remove the pouch from the loom and turn right side out.

10 The pouch is complete.

Flat Loom Weaving Tips

When Weaving Fine Yarn

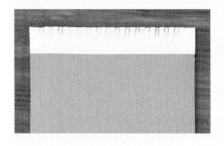

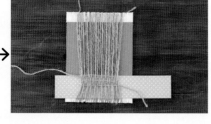

Cut More Notches in the Loom

Add an extra notch positioned between each corrugated cardboard line. This means that the notches will be positioned at ⅛-¼ in (4-5 mm) intervals.

Weave Guide Rows

Weave 3-4 rows using a non-stretch yarn, such as the hemp cord pictured here. Pull the tails to narrow the width of the warp threads, drawing them closer together than it is possible to cut notches. Use a fork to adjust the space between warp threads based on the thickness of the weft yarn to be used. Once you begin weaving with the actual weft yarn, remove the guide rows. This is known as loom waste.

When Weaving Torn Fabric Strips

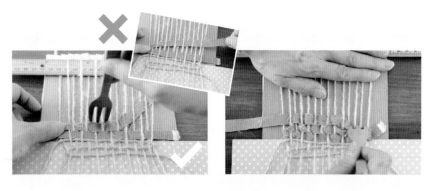

Don't Tug on Torn Fabric Strips

If you tug on the torn fabric strip too tightly, you will pull in the warp threads. Pretty soon you'll find that your weaving is becoming too narrow. Instead, use your thumb to hold the intersection of the warp and weft as you pack the fabric strip down with a fork. This will allow the fabric strip to settle in, and not pull in at the sides.

Weave Guide Rows

When weaving with torn fabric strips, weave a few guide rows to adjust the space between warp threads, just like when weaving with fine yarn. After weaving 2-3 rows, pack down the weave using a fork. Make sure to hold the warp threads in place with your other hand.

How to Add Weft Yarn

Torn fabric strips can be difficult to handle if they're too long. Instead, weave using 24-40 in (60-100 cm) long strips. When it's time to add a new strip, overlap ⅜ in (1 cm) and glue to the end of the old strip.

BOX LOOM

As the name suggests, these looms are made from cardboard boxes. You'll weave around the circumference of the box to create three-dimensional items with a tubular shape, which can be used to create cowls, hats, and bags.

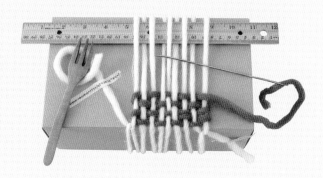

HOW TO MAKE A BOX LOOM

Tools & Materials

- Cardboard box

The only thing you need to do to make this loom is to locate an appropriately sized cardboard box for your weaving project. If you're having trouble finding a suitable box, there are a few things you can do:

If your box is too short: Make your box taller by adding some books or a few layers of cardboard until you achieve the desired height.

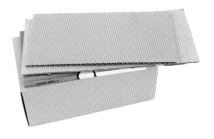

If your box is too big: Cut the box to make it smaller.

If you can't find a box: Cut a piece of flat cardboard to the required size and fold it into a box shape, then tape or glue in place.

HOW TO WEAVE ON A BOX LOOM

String the Loom

1 Starting at a corner of the box, wrap the warp thread around the box once and knot, leaving a 4 in (10 cm) long tail.

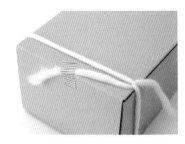

2 Use masking tape to secure the warp thread tail to the side of the box.

3 Continue wrapping the warp threads around the box until they measure ⅜-⅝ in (1-1.5 cm) wider than the desired finished width of the textile.

4 Once the wraps are complete, make a knot along the same side as in step 1. Trim the excess yarn, leaving a 4 in (10 cm) long tail.

5 Use masking tape to secure the warp thread tail from step 4. Count to make sure you have the same number of warp threads on all sides of the box.

6 Adjust the warp threads so they are evenly spaced about ⅜ in (1 cm) apart. Insert a ruler under and over alternating warp threads. This will be shed stick B.

Weave the Weft Thread

7 Thread a weaving needle with a 1-2 yd (1-2 m) long piece of weft thread. Start weaving on the side of the box with the knot. Raise the ruler and insert the needle from right to left.

8 Leave a 2 in (5 cm) long thread tail, then use a fork to align the weft row with the edge of the box. The first row is complete.

9 Starting from the left edge of the loom, insert the weaving needle over and under the opposite warp threads as in step 7.

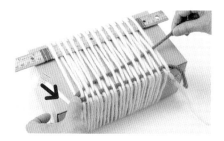

10 Use your thumb to hold the intersection of the warp and weft as you pull the weft down into place.

11 Slide the ruler down to pack down the weave. It may also help to use a fork. Two rows are now complete.

12 Repeat steps 7-11 to continue weaving around the box. When you reach a corner, slide the ruler to the next side of the box, then continue weaving.

13 When you approach the end, there will no longer be space left for the ruler. Switch the ruler out for a knitting needle (shed stick A) and continue to weave.

14 For the final row, make sure that the weft thread passes under and over the opposite warp threads as the first row woven in step 7.

15 Weave the weft thread end over and under a few warp threads following the same pattern as in the first weft row. Follow the same process to weave in the weft thread tail left in step 8.

Finish the Textile

16 Remove the pieces of masking tape holding the warp thread tails in place, then remove the textile from the loom. You will have a tube-shaped textile.

17 Use a crochet hook to bring the weft thread tails from step 15 to the wrong side. Hide the warp thread tails under a few stitches on the wrong side and trim. You can also use the warp thread tails to seam the textile if required.

18 The textile is complete.

Box Loom Weaving Tips

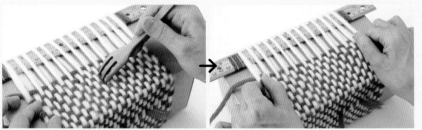

How to Weave at the Corners

As you approach the corner, slide the ruler to the edge of the box and lift it up to create space between the warp threads.

How to Adjust the Tension

As you continue the weave, the stitches tend to become rather tight. When this happens, use a fork to spread out the stitches, then hold both edges of the textile and gently stretch to reduce the tension.

How to Transform a Tube-Shaped Textile Into a Hat or Bag

After removing the textile from the loom, pull the warp thread tail to gather the tube.

Use the warp thread tail to sew the gathered end closed for a hat. To make a bag, loosen the gathers slightly and adjust to achieve the proper size and silhouette before sewing closed.

POTHOLDER & TRIVET SET

Shown on page 7

FOR THE POTHOLDERS (SET OF 2)

FIBER

- **Warp:** 33 yds (31 m) of navy hemp cord
- **Weft:** 8 x 43 ¼ in (20 x 110 cm) each of red plaid flannel fabric, navy plaid flannel fabric, and blue and white houndstooth flannel fabric

OTHER MATERIALS

- Craft glue
- Sewing thread

FINISHED PROJECT SIZE

4 ¼ x 7 in (11 x 18 cm)

LOOM USED

Table loom: 7 in (18 cm) or wider

INSTRUCTIONS

1. Make a table loom, as shown on page 40. Refer to the strung length listed below when positioning the loom.

2. String the loom according to the specifications listed below. Note: You will be weaving both potholders at once.

Number of Warp Threads: 16 (1 strand each)
Strung Width: 5 ¼ in (13 cm)
Strung Length: 39 ½ in (100 cm)

3. Insert a 2 ⅜ in (6 cm) wide header to mark the fringe placement along the bottom of the loom, as shown on page 42.

4. Use hemp cord to weave three guide rows, as shown on page 58. Pull the tails to adjust the width of the warp threads to 4 ¼ in (11 cm).

5. Prepare the weft thread by cutting the fabric into strips measuring ½ x 43 ¼ in (1.2 x 110 cm). Glue strips of the same fabric together, as shown on page 58.

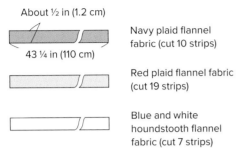

About ½ in (1.2 cm)

43 ¼ in (110 cm)

Navy plaid flannel fabric (cut 10 strips)

Red plaid flannel fabric (cut 19 strips)

Blue and white houndstooth flannel fabric (cut 7 strips)

6. To create the first potholder, weave for 13 ½ in (34 cm) following Color Scheme A (refer to page 43 for table loom weaving instructions).

Weft Color Schemes

A

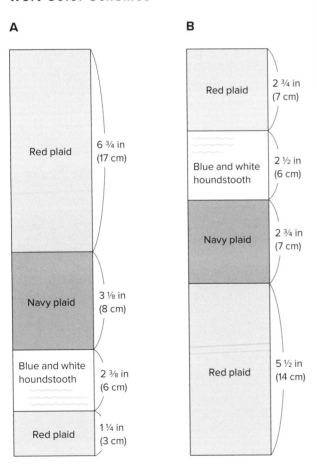

Red plaid — 6 ¾ in (17 cm)

Navy plaid — 3 ⅛ in (8 cm)

Blue and white houndstooth — 2 ⅜ in (6 cm)

Red plaid — 1 ¼ in (3 cm)

B

Red plaid — 2 ¾ in (7 cm)

Blue and white houndstooth — 2 ½ in (6 cm)

Navy plaid — 2 ¾ in (7 cm)

Red plaid — 5 ½ in (14 cm)

7. Next, leave about 8 in (20 cm) of space, then create the second potholder by weaving for 13 ½ in (34 cm) following Color Scheme B shown in step 6.

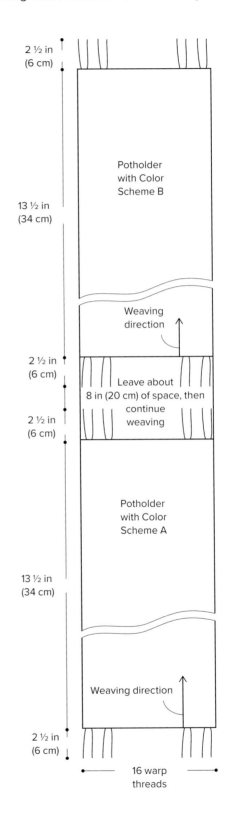

2 ½ in (6 cm)

13 ½ in (34 cm)

Potholder with Color Scheme B

Weaving direction

2 ½ in (6 cm)

Leave about 8 in (20 cm) of space, then continue weaving

2 ½ in (6 cm)

Potholder with Color Scheme A

13 ½ in (34 cm)

Weaving direction

2 ½ in (6 cm)

16 warp threads

8. Cut the 8 in (20 cm) space in half to separate the two potholders. Use Method B on page 46 to create fringe using the warp threads.

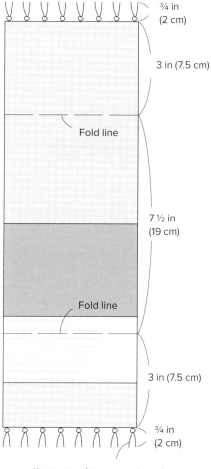

¾ in (2 cm)

3 in (7.5 cm)

Fold line

7 ½ in (19 cm)

Fold line

3 in (7.5 cm)

¾ in (2 cm)

Knot sets of two warp threads together, then trim to ¾ in (2 cm)

9. Weave in the weft thread tails, as shown on page 44.

10. Fold each potholder along the lines noted in the step 8 diagram. Whipstitch the two layers together along the left and right edges to create pockets. Finally, insert a 6 in (15 cm) long piece of hemp cord through a couple stitches on an edge of each potholder and tie into a loop.

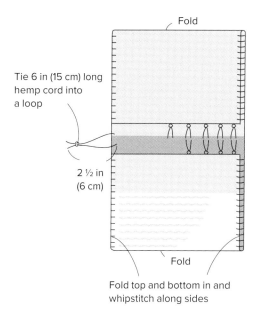

Fold

Tie 6 in (15 cm) long hemp cord into a loop

2 ½ in (6 cm)

Fold

Fold top and bottom in and whipstitch along sides

Finished Diagram

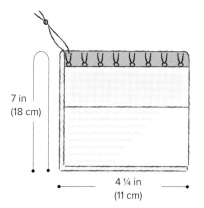

7 in (18 cm)

4 ¼ in (11 cm)

FOR THE TRIVET

FIBER

Warp: 16 yds (15 m) of navy hemp cord

Weft: 3 ⅛ x 43 ¼ in (8 x 110 cm) each of red plaid flannel fabric, navy plaid flannel fabric, and blue and white houndstooth flannel fabric

OTHER MATERIALS

- Craft glue

FINISHED PROJECT SIZE

8 in (20 cm) diameter without fringe

LOOM USED

Flat loom for round weaving: 13 in (33 cm) square

INSTRUCTIONS

1. Make a flat loom for round weaving, as shown on page 50. You'll cut 33 notches on each side of the loom.

2. String the loom according to the diagram below. You should have a total of 44 warp threads. Before you begin weaving, you'll need to bundle two warp threads together to create an odd number, as shown in step 6 on page 51.

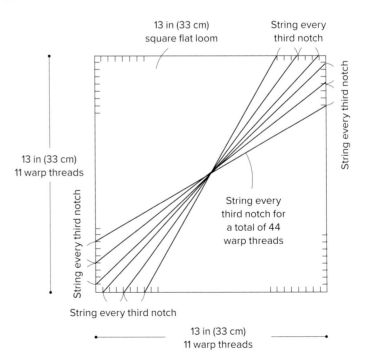

13 in (33 cm) square flat loom

String every third notch

String every third notch

13 in (33 cm) 11 warp threads

String every third notch for a total of 44 warp threads

String every third notch

String every third notch

13 in (33 cm) 11 warp threads

3. Prepare the weft thread by cutting the fabric into strips, measuring ½ x 43 ¼ in (1.2 x 110 cm). Glue the strips together, alternating the three fabrics as shown.

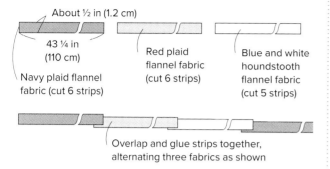

About ½ in (1.2 cm)

43 ¼ in (110 cm)

Navy plaid flannel fabric (cut 6 strips)

Red plaid flannel fabric (cut 6 strips)

Blue and white houndstooth flannel fabric (cut 5 strips)

Overlap and glue strips together, alternating three fabrics as shown

4. Start weaving as shown on page 51, leaving a 3 ⅛ in (8 cm) long weft thread tail. Weave until the textile measures slightly over 8 in (20 cm) in diameter.

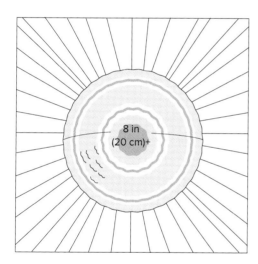

8 in (20 cm)+

5. Use the warp threads to make fringe, as shown on page 52, but leave one warp thread as a short loop to be used for hanging the potholder.

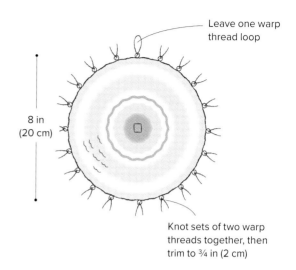

Leave one warp thread loop

8 in (20 cm)

Knot sets of two warp threads together, then trim to ¾ in (2 cm)

6. Weave in the weft thread tails, as shown on page 52.

LINEN COASTERS

Shown on page 6

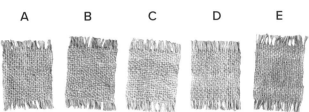

A   B   C   D   E

FIBER

Use bulky linen yarn for warp and weft in the following color combinations:

Plaid Variations

A
- **Main color:** 14 yds (13 m) of blue
- **Accent color:** 7 yds (6.5 m) of orange

C
- **Main color:** 14 yds (13 m) of white
- **Accent color:** 7 yds (6.5 m) of blue

D
- **Main color:** 14 yds (13 m) of orange
- **Accent color:** 7 yds (6.5 m) of white

Striped Variations

B
- **Main color:** 14 yds (13 m) of orange
- **Accent color:** 7 yds (6.5 m) of blue

E
- **Main color:** 14 yds (13 m) of blue
- **Accent color:** 7 yds (6.5 m) of white

OTHER MATERIALS

- Fabric glue

FINISHED PROJECT SIZE

4 x 5 ½ in (10 x 14 cm) including fringe

LOOM USED

Flat loom: 6 in (15 cm) wide x 8 in (20 cm) long

INSTRUCTIONS

1. Make a basic flat loom, as shown on page 48, but cut an extra notch between each corrugated cardboard line, as shown on page 58.

2. String the loom according to the specifications listed below. For the plaid variations, follow the warp color scheme shown in the step 5 diagram on page 69.

> **Number of Warp Threads:** 26 (1 strand each)
> **Strung Width:** 4 ¼ in (11 cm)
> **Strung Length:** 8 in (20 cm)

3. Insert a 2 in (5 cm) wide header to mark the fringe placement along the bottom of the loom, as shown on page 49.

4. Use hemp cord to weave three guide rows, as shown on page 58. Pull the tails to adjust the width of the warp threads to 4 in (10 cm).

5. Use one strand of weft thread to weave for 4 in (10 cm), as shown on page 49, packing down the rows as you work so there are no gaps.

Plaid Variations

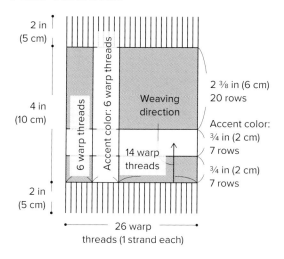

2 in (5 cm)

4 in (10 cm)

2 in (5 cm)

6 warp threads

Accent color: 6 warp threads

Weaving direction

14 warp threads

2 3/8 in (6 cm) 20 rows

Accent color: 3/4 in (2 cm) 7 rows

3/4 in (2 cm) 7 rows

26 warp threads (1 strand each)

	Accent Color	Main Color
A	Orange	Blue
C	Blue	White
D	White	Orange

Striped Variations

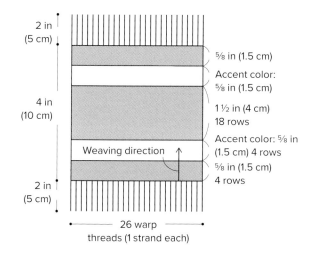

2 in (5 cm)

4 in (10 cm)

2 in (5 cm)

Weaving direction

5/8 in (1.5 cm)

Accent color: 5/8 in (1.5 cm)

1 1/2 in (4 cm) 18 rows

Accent color: 5/8 in (1.5 cm) 4 rows

5/8 in (1.5 cm) 4 rows

26 warp threads (1 strand each)

	Accent Color	Main Color
B	Blue	Orange
E	White	Blue

6. Use Method A on page 46 to create fringe using the warp threads.

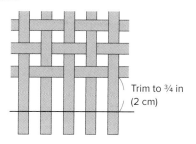

Trim to 3/4 in (2 cm)

Finished Diagrams

Plaid Variations

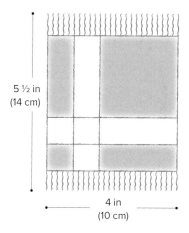

5 1/2 in (14 cm)

4 in (10 cm)

Striped Variations

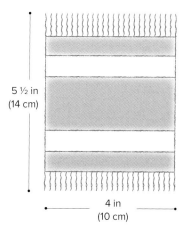

5 1/2 in (14 cm)

4 in (10 cm)

ROUND SEAT CUSHIONS

Shown on page 8

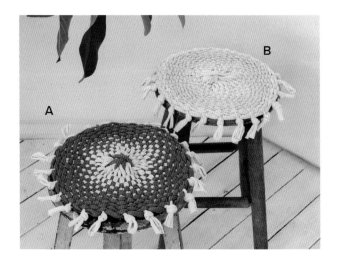

FIBER

Use super bulky t-shirt yarn, such as Hoooked Zpagetti, in the following color combinations:

A
- **Warp:** 24 yds (22 m) in light blue
- **Weft:** 24 yds (22 m) in red

B
- **Warp (plus a little weft):** 24 yds (22 m) in pink
- **Weft:** 24 yds (22 m) in light blue

OTHER MATERIALS

- Craft glue
- Sewing thread

FINISHED PROJECT SIZE

11 in (28 cm) diameter without fringe

LOOM USED

Flat loom for round weaving:
18 ¼ in (46 cm) square

Tip: It may help to use a safety pin or a scrap of yarn tied into a bow to hold the warp threads together at the center of the loom. Once the weaving gets going, the center warp threads should stay in place.

INSTRUCTIONS

1. Make a flat loom for round weaving, as shown on page 50. You'll cut 48 notches on each side of the loom.

2. String the loom according to the diagram below. You should have a total of 48 warp threads. Before you begin weaving, you'll need to bundle two warp threads together to create an odd number, as shown in step 6 on page 51.

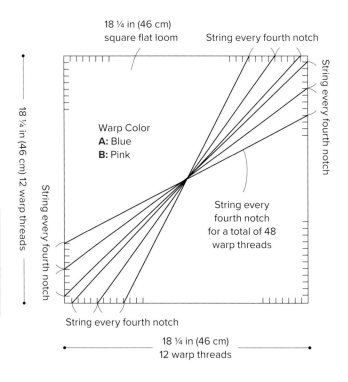

18 ¼ in (46 cm) square flat loom

String every fourth notch

String every fourth notch

18 ¼ in (46 cm) 12 warp threads

String every fourth notch

Warp Color
A: Blue
B: Pink

String every fourth notch for a total of 48 warp threads

String every fourth notch

18 ¼ in (46 cm)
12 warp threads

3. Using one strand of weft thread, weave the first round, leaving a 6 in (15 cm) long tail. Do not tighten the first round, as this may distort the weave.

4. For A, weave until the textile measures 12 ¾ in (32 cm) in diameter, as shown on page 51. For B, use the blue yarn to weave until the textile measures about 11 ¾ in (30 cm) in diameter, then use the pink yarn to weave three more rows.

5. Weave in the weft thread tails and use the warp threads to make fringe, as shown on page 52 and the diagram below.

6. Use sewing thread to sew the warp threads together at the center of the textile so they lie flat, as shown in the diagram below.

7. Next, use a scrap of weft thread to stitch a flower shape at the center of the textile, covering the sewing thread from step 6, as shown in the diagram below.

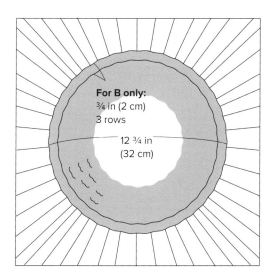

For B only:
¾ in (2 cm)
3 rows

12 ¾ in
(32 cm)

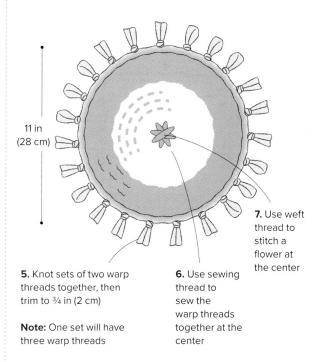

11 in
(28 cm)

5. Knot sets of two warp threads together, then trim to ¾ in (2 cm)

Note: One set will have three warp threads

6. Use sewing thread to sew the warp threads together at the center

7. Use weft thread to stitch a flower at the center

Tip: T-shirt yarn is very stretchy, so if you string the loom too tightly, your textile will shrink considerably when you remove it from the loom. Take care to string the loom at the proper tension and weave a bit looser than normal when working with t-shirt yarn.

SQUARE SEAT CUSHIONS

Shown on page 9

FIBER

Use super bulky t-shirt yarn, such as Hoooked Zpagetti, in the following color combinations:

A
- **Both Warp & Weft:** 19 yds (18 m) in gray
- **Weft:** 19 yds (18 m) in red

B
- **Both Warp & Weft:** 19 yds (18 m) in pink
- **Weft:** 19 yds (18 m) in floral print

C
- **Both Warp & Weft:** 19 yds (18 m) in gray
- **Weft:** 19 yds (18 m) in green print

FINISHED PROJECT SIZE

11 ½ x 11 ½ in (29 x 29 cm)

LOOM USED

Flat loom: 13 in (33 cm) square

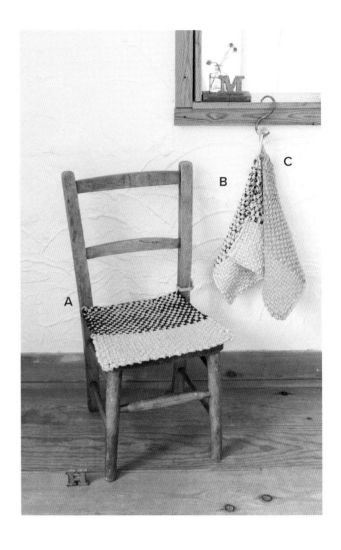

INSTRUCTIONS

1. Make a basic flat loom, as shown on page 48.

2. String the loom according to the specifications listed below.

> **Number of Warp Threads:** 36 (1 strand each)
> **Strung Width:** 13 in (33 cm)
> **Strung Length:** 13 in (33 cm)

3. Using one strand of weft thread, loosely weave the first row, leaving a 6 in (15 cm) long tail.

4. Weave for 13 in (33 cm), as noted in the diagram below, using the no fringe Method C on page 47 to finish the thread tails as you work (refer to page 49 for flat loom weaving instructions).

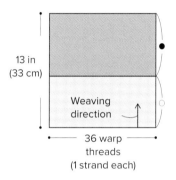

13 in (33 cm)

Weaving direction

36 warp threads (1 strand each)

5. Thread an 8 in (20 cm) long scrap of yarn through the corner of the cushion, tie into a loop, and trim the ends to ⅜ in (1 cm).

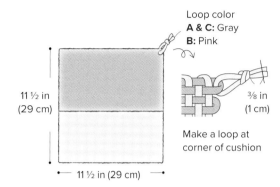

11 ½ in (29 cm)

11 ½ in (29 cm)

Loop color
A & C: Gray
B: Pink

⅜ in (1 cm)

Make a loop at corner of cushion

Tip: T-shirt yarn is very stretchy, so if you string the loom too tightly, your textile will shrink considerably when you remove it from the loom. Take care to string the loom at the proper tension and weave a bit looser than normal when working with t-shirt yarn.

Variation	○	●
A	Gray 15 rows	Red 17 rows
B	Pink 16 rows	Floral print 16 rows
C	Gray 10 rows	Green print 22 rows

BUTTONED UP PILLOW SHAMS

Shown on page 10

FIBER

A

- **Both Warp & Weft:** 54 yds (49 m) of super bulky slub wool yarn in brick red

B

- **Both Warp & Weft:** 54 yds (49 m) of super bulky slub wool yarn in mustard yellow

C

Both Warp & Weft:

- 54 yds (49 m) of super bulky slub wool yarn in light blue
- 72 yds (65 m) of fine pom-pom novelty yarn in blue

OTHER MATERIALS

- Three ¾ in (2.2 cm) diameter buttons
- Sewing thread
- Pillow form

FINISHED PROJECT SIZE

12 ¼ in (31 cm) square

LOOM USED

Box loom: At least 13 ¾ in (35 cm) wide with a 26 ¾ in (68 cm) circumference

INSTRUCTIONS

1. Locate a box matching the size requirements listed on page 74 or make your own box loom, as shown on page 59.

2. String the loom according to the specifications listed below.

> **Number of Warp Threads:** 41 (**A & B:** 1 strand each, **C:** 1 strand of super bulky slub wool + 1 strand of fine pom-pom novelty yarn)
> **Strung Width:** 12 ¾ in (32 cm)
> **Strung Length:** 26 ¾ in (68 cm)

3. Start weaving as shown on page 60, leaving a good size weft thread tail. Weave around the circumference of the box.

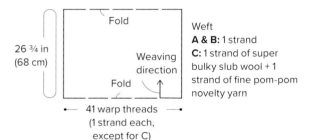

4. Remove the textile from the loom. Use the weft thread tail from step 3 to whipstitch the end of the sham closed. On the other end of the sham, sew three buttons to the inside bottom layer.

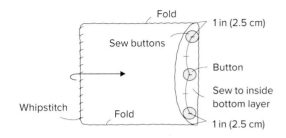

5. Insert a pillow form into the sham. Insert the buttons through the weave of the top layer of the sham to secure.

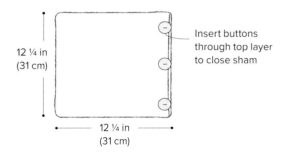

TISSUE BOX COZY

Shown on page 12

FIBER

Both Warp & Weft

- 66 yds (61 m) of bulky wool yarn in teal, such as Álafoss Lopi

Warp

- 33 yds (31 m) of bulky wool yarn in ivory, such as Álafoss Lopi

OTHER MATERIALS

- Two ¾ in (2 cm) diameter buttons
- Sewing thread

FINISHED PROJECT SIZE

4 ¾ x 12 ¼ x 2 ¼ in (12 x 31 x 5.5 cm)

LOOM USED

Table loom: 15 in (38 cm) or wider

INSTRUCTIONS

1. Make a table loom, as shown on page 40. Refer to the strung length listed below when positioning the loom.

2. String the loom according to the specifications listed below. Follow the warp color scheme shown below:

> **Number of Warp Threads:** 44 (2 strands each)
> **Strung Width:** 14 ¾ in (36 cm)
> **Strung Length:** 21 in (53 cm)

Warp Color Scheme

Teal	Ivory	Teal
9 threads	26 threads	9 threads

3. Insert a 2 in (5 cm) wide header to mark the fringe placement along the bottom of the loom, as shown on page 42.

4. Using two strands of weft thread, weave for 17 in (43 cm), as shown on page 43.

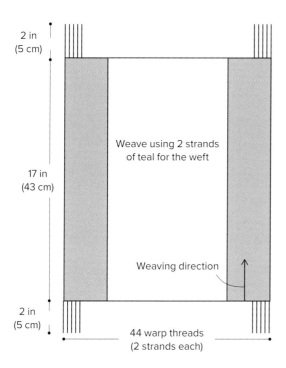

2 in (5 cm)

17 in (43 cm)

Weave using 2 strands of teal for the weft

Weaving direction

2 in (5 cm)

44 warp threads (2 strands each)

5. Use Method B on page 46 to create fringe using the warp threads.

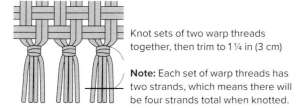

Knot sets of two warp threads together, then trim to 1 ¼ in (3 cm)

Note: Each set of warp threads has two strands, which means there will be four strands total when knotted.

6. Fold the textile in half, aligning the fringe. Use a scrap of teal yarn to sew the two layers together, leaving a large opening at the center.

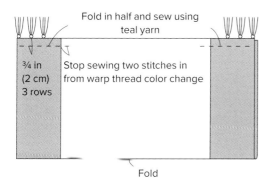

Fold in half and sew using teal yarn

¾ in (2 cm) 3 rows

Stop sewing two stitches in from warp thread color change

Fold

7. Press the seam allowance from step 6 open. Use a scrap of teal yarn to stitch the seam allowance in place along the opening edges of the top layer only.

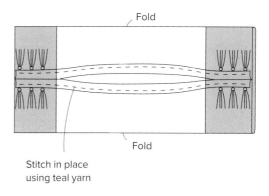

Fold

Fold

Stitch in place using teal yarn

8. Sew a button to each end on the top layer of the cozy. Use scraps of teal yarn to make corresponding loops on the bottom layer of the cozy. Use the buttons and loops to secure a tissue box inside the cozy.

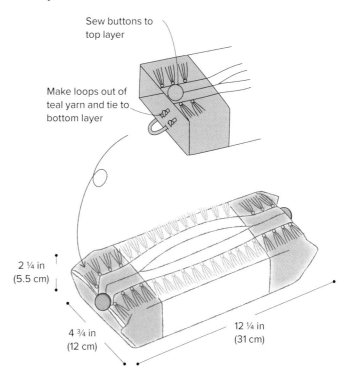

Sew buttons to top layer

Make loops out of teal yarn and tie to bottom layer

2 ¼ in (5.5 cm)

4 ¾ in (12 cm)

12 ¼ in (31 cm)

STRIPED FLOOR MAT

Shown on page 13

FIBER

Warp
- 91 yds (84 m) of DK acrylic/jute blend yarn

Weft
- 11 ¾ x 43 ¼ in (30 x 110 cm) of red and beige striped cotton/linen blend fabric
- 3 ⅛ x 45 ¼ in (8 x 115 cm) of blue denim fabric
- 4 ¾ x 23 ¾ in (12 x 60 cm) of beige linen fabric

OTHER MATERIALS

- Fabric glue

FINISHED PROJECT SIZE

13 x 23 ¼ in (33 x 59 cm) including fringe

LOOM USED

Table loom: 18 in (45 cm) or wider

INSTRUCTIONS

1. Make a table loom, as shown on page 40. Refer to the strung length listed below when positioning the loom.

2. String the loom according to the specifications listed below:

> **Number of Warp Threads:** 48 (3 strands each)
> **Strung Width:** 15 ¾ in (40 cm)
> **Strung Length:** 25 ½ in (65 cm)

3. Insert a 3 ⅛ in (8 cm) wide header at the bottom of the loom to mark the fringe placement, as shown on page 42.

4. Prepare the weft threads by cutting the fabric into strips and gluing the strips together.

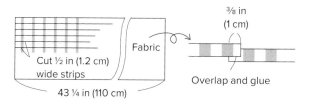

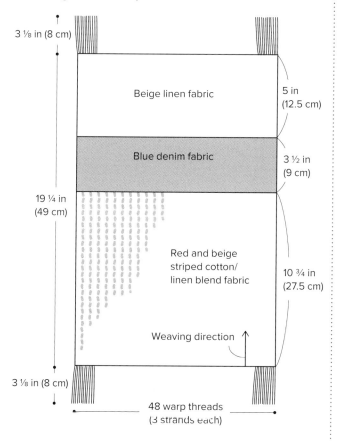

Experiment with pattern when cutting your fabric into strips. If you're using striped fabric, cut in the same direction to preserve the stripes, or cut in a crosswise direction to create a checkered pattern when woven.

5. Weave for 19 ¼ in (49 cm), following the layout noted below (refer to page 43 for table loom weaving instructions).

6. Use Method B on page 46 to create fringe using the warp threads.

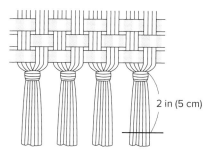

Bundle the warp threads into groups of 6 strands. Knot together, then trim the fringe to 2 in (5 cm)

Finished Diagram

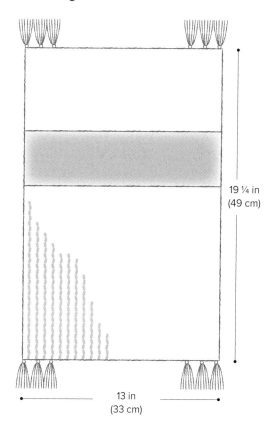

FAUX FUR STOLE

Shown on page 17

FIBER

Both Warp & Weft
- 55 yds (51 m) of bulky furry novelty yarn in beige

OTHER TOOLS & MATERIALS

- Four ⅜ in (1 cm) diameter pearl beads
- Craft glue
- Scrap of wire
- J-10 (6.0 mm) crochet hook

FINISHED PROJECT SIZE

5 ¼ x 19 ¾ in (13 x 50 cm)

LOOM USED

Table loom: 6 in (15 cm) or wider

INSTRUCTIONS

1. Make a table loom, as shown on page 40. Refer to the strung length listed below when positioning the loom.

2. String the loom according to the specifications below. String 1 ½ yd (1.4 m) long pieces of yarn through the second and third sets of notches in from the left edge of the loom. These will become the ties.

> **Number of Warp Threads:** 15 (1 strand each)
> **Strung Width:** 5 ¼ in (13.5 cm)
> **Strung Length:** 21 ¼ in (54 cm)

3. Using two strands of weft thread, weave for 21 ¼ in (54 cm) using the no fringe Method C on page 47 (refer to page 43 for table loom weaving instructions).

4. Use a crochet hook to chain stitch each tie, leaving 2 in (5 cm) of yarn at the end of each tie.

5. Fold the scrap of wire into a V-shape. Use it to pull each tie through a pearl bead, then knot the end of each tie. Apply a dab of glue to secure each bead to its knot. Once the glue is dry, trim the excess yarn.

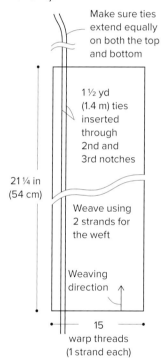

Make sure ties extend equally on both the top and bottom

1 ½ yd (1.4 m) ties inserted through 2nd and 3rd notches

21 ¼ in (54 cm)

Weave using 2 strands for the weft

Weaving direction

15 warp threads (1 strand each)

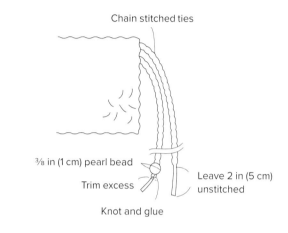

Chain stitched ties

⅜ in (1 cm) pearl bead

Trim excess

Leave 2 in (5 cm) unstitched

Knot and glue

Finished Diagram

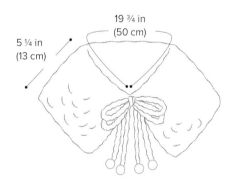

19 ¾ in (50 cm)

5 ¼ in (13 cm)

BOUCLÉ SCARF

Shown on page 15

FIBER

Both Warp & Weft:
- 77 yds (71 m) of super bulky bouclé yarn

OTHER MATERIALS

- Fabric glue

FINISHED PROJECT SIZE

5 ½ x 45 in (14 x 114 cm) including fringe

LOOM USED

Table loom: 7 in (18 cm) or wider

INSTRUCTIONS

1. Make a table loom, as shown on page 40. Refer to the strung length listed below when positioning the loom.

2. String the loom according to the specifications listed below.

> **Number of Warp Threads:** 17 (1 strand each)
> **Strung Width:** 5 ¾ in (14.5 cm)
> **Strung Length:** 47 ¼ in (120 cm)

3. Insert a 2 in (5 cm) wide header along the bottom of the loom to mark the fringe placement, as shown on page 42.

4. Using two strands of yarn held together as the weft thread, weave for 43 ¼ in (110 cm), as shown on page 43.

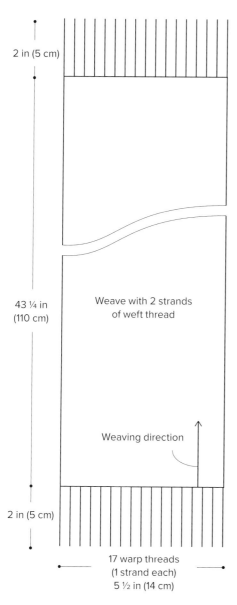

2 in (5 cm)

43 ¼ in (110 cm)

Weave with 2 strands of weft thread

Weaving direction

2 in (5 cm)

17 warp threads (1 strand each) 5 ½ in (14 cm)

5. Trim the warp threads as shown.

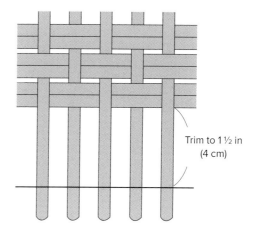

Trim to 1 ½ in (4 cm)

6. Use Method A on page 46 to create fringe using the warp threads.

AUTUMN SKY SCARF

Shown on page 14

Shown on page 14

FIBER

Both Warp & Weft:

- 230 yds (211 m) of aran wool/mohair blend yarn

OTHER MATERIALS

- Fabric glue

FINISHED PROJECT SIZE

5 ½ x 45 ¼ in (14 x 115 cm) including fringe

LOOM USED

Table loom: 8 in (20 cm) or wider

INSTRUCTIONS

1. Make a table loom, as shown on page 40. Refer to the strung length listed below when positioning the loom.

2. String the loom according to the specifications listed below.

> **Number of Warp Threads:** 20 (2 strands each)
> **Strung Width:** 6 ¾ in (17 cm)
> **Strung Length:** 47 ¼ in (120 cm)

3. Insert a 2 in (5 cm) wide header along the bottom of the loom to mark the fringe placement, as shown on page 42.

4. Using two strands of yarn held together as the weft thread, weave for 43 ¼ in (110 cm), as shown on page 43.

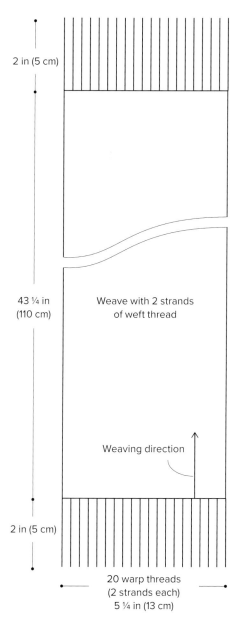

2 in (5 cm)

43 ¼ in
(110 cm)

Weave with 2 strands
of weft thread

Weaving direction

2 in (5 cm)

20 warp threads
(2 strands each)
5 ¼ in (13 cm)

5. Trim the warp threads as shown.

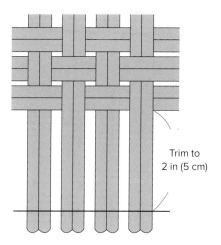

Trim to
2 in (5 cm)

6. Use Method A on page 46 to create fringe using the warp threads.

SCALLOPED SCARF

Shown on page 18

FIBER

Both Warp & Weft
- 73 yds (67 m) of aran loop novelty yarn in green

FINISHED PROJECT SIZE

4 ¼ x 48 ½ in (11 x 123 cm)

LOOM USED

Table loom: 6 in (15 cm) or wider

INSTRUCTIONS

1. Make a table loom, as shown on page 40. Refer to the strung length listed below when positioning the loom.

2. String the loom according to the specifications listed below.

> **Number of Warp Threads:** 13 (1 strand each)
> **Strung Width:** 4 ¾ in (12 cm)
> **Strung Length:** 51 ¼ in (130 cm)

3. Using one strand of weft thread, start weaving using the no fringe Method C on page 47 (refer to page 43 for table loom weaving instructions).

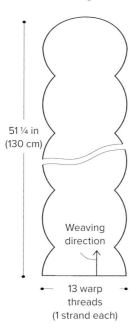

51 ¼ in
(130 cm)

Weaving
direction

13 warp
threads
(1 strand each)

4. Adjust the tightness every 9-12 rows to create a scalloped shape. The scarf should measure 2 ¾ in (7 cm) at the narrowest points and 4 ¼ in (11 cm) at the widest points. Weave until the scarf measures 51 ¼ in (130 cm) long.

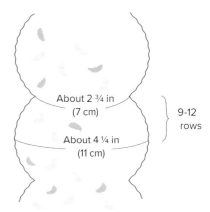

About 2 ¾ in
(7 cm)

9-12
rows

About 4 ¼ in
(11 cm)

Weave using 1 strand
for the weft, adjusting
the tightness to create
scalloped shape

BLOOMING FLOWERS SCARF

Shown on page 19

FIBER

Warp

- 77 yds (71 m) of silk/nylon sport bouclé yarn in almond
- 23 yds (22 m) of cotton/silk ladder novelty yarn in beige
- 44 yds (41 m) of cotton/nylon sport slub loop yarn in beige
- 175 yds (160 m) of bulky pom-pom yarn in red
- 103 yds (95 m) of lace flag novelty yarn in rose

Warp & Weft

- 350 yds (320 m) of cotton DK eyelash yarn in camel

Weft

- 77 yds (71 m) wool/nylon loop novelty yarn in light brown

FINISHED PROJECT SIZE

6 ¼ x 49 ¾ in (16 x 126 cm)

LOOM USED

Table loom: 8 ¾ in (22 cm) or wider

INSTRUCTIONS

1. Make a table loom, as shown on page 40. Refer to the strung length listed below when positioning the loom.

2. String the loom according to the specifications listed below. Follow the warp color scheme shown below:

> **Number of Warp Threads:** 20 (2-3 strands each, as noted below)
> **Strung Width:** 7 in (18 cm)
> **Strung Length:** 55 in (140 cm)

Warp Color Scheme

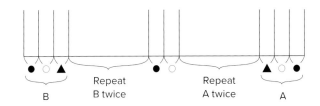

● = 3 strands total
{ Bouclé
  Ladder
  Eyelash

○ = 2 strands total
{ Bouclé
  Slub loop

▲ = 3 strands total
{ Flag
  Pom-pom
  Bouclé

3. Insert a 2 ¾ in (7 cm) wide header to mark the fringe placement along the bottom of the loom, as shown on page 42.

4. Using two strands of weft thread (one strand of eyelash yarn and one strand of wool/nylon loop novelty yarn), weave loosely for 49 ¾ in (126 cm). You should have about three rows every ¾ in (2 cm). Refer to page 43 for table loom weaving instructions.

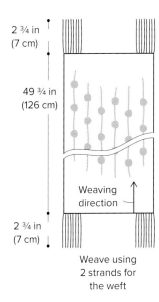

2 ¾ in (7 cm)

49 ¾ in (126 cm)

Weaving direction

2 ¾ in (7 cm)

Weave using 2 strands for the weft

5. Use Method B on page 46 to create fringe using the warp threads.

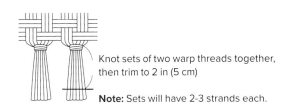

Knot sets of two warp threads together, then trim to 2 in (5 cm)

Note: Sets will have 2-3 strands each.

RIBBON SCARF

Shown on page 16

FIBER

Warp & Weft
- 100 yds (92 m) of DK wool tweed yarn in pink

Warp
- One 47 in (119 cm) piece of ½ in (1 cm) wide velvet ribbon in fuchsia
- One 47 in (119 cm) piece of ⅜ in (8 mm) wide velvet ribbon in sage green
- Three 47 in (119 cm) pieces of ⅛ in (3 mm) wide velvet ribbon in beige
- Two 47 in (119 cm) pieces of ¼ in (6 mm) wide rickrack in beige
- Two 47 in (119 cm) pieces of ¼ in (6 mm) wide rickrack in light blue

OTHER MATERIALS

- Fabric glue

FINISHED PROJECT SIZE

4 ¾ x 42 ¼ in (12 x 107 cm) including fringe

LOOM USED

Table loom: 8 in (20 cm) or wider

INSTRUCTIONS

1. Make a table loom, as shown on page 40. Refer to the strung length listed below when positioning the loom.

2. String the loom according to the specifications listed below. Follow the warp color scheme shown below. If the ribbon or rickrack will not stay in the notches, use masking tape to secure it to the back of the loom.

> **Number of Warp Threads:** 19 (3 strands of yarn = 1 warp thread, while 1 strand of ribbon/rickrack = 1 warp thread)
> **Strung Width:** 6 ¼ in (16 cm)
> **Strung Length:** 45 ¼ in (115 cm)

Warp Color Scheme

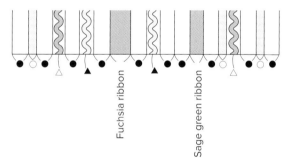

▲ = Beige rickrack
△ = Light blue rickrack
● = Pink yarn (3 strands)
○ = Beige velvet ribbon

3. Insert a 2 in (5 cm) wide header to mark the fringe placement along the bottom of the loom, as shown on page 42.

4. Using two strands of weft thread, weave for 41 ¼ in (105 cm), as shown on page 43.

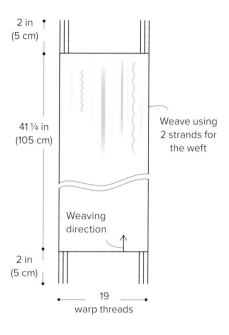

5. Use Method A on page 46 to create fringe using the warp threads.

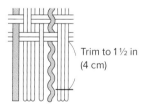

SUEDE STRIPED SCARF

Shown on page 20

FIBER

Warp
- 33 yds (31 m) of bulky wool in light gray, such as Álafoss Lopi
- Four 48 ¾ in (124 cm) pieces of ¼ in (6 mm) wide brown leather cord

Weft
- 50 yds (46 m) of bulky wool in moss green, such as Álafoss Lopi

OTHER MATERIALS

- Fabric glue
- Craft glue

FINISHED PROJECT SIZE

5 ¼ x 45 ¼ in (13 x 115 cm) including fringe

LOOM USED

Table loom: 6 ¾ in (17 cm) or wider

INSTRUCTIONS

1. Make a table loom, as shown on page 40. Refer to the strung length listed below when positioning the loom.

2. String the loom according to the specifications listed below. Follow the warp color scheme shown below.

Warp Color Scheme

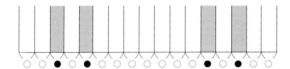

○ = Light gray yarn
(2 strands each)

● = Suede cord
(1 strand each)

If your pieces of suede cord aren't long enough, overlap and glue them together to reach desired length

Number of Warp Threads: 17 (2 strands of yarn = 1 warp thread, while 1 strand of suede cord = 1 warp thread)
Strung Width: 6 in (15 cm)
Strung Length: 47 ¼ in (120 cm)

3. Insert a 2 in (5 cm) wide header to mark the fringe placement along the bottom of the loom, as shown on page 42.

4. Using two strands of weft thread, weave for 43 ¼ in 110 cm), as shown on page 43.

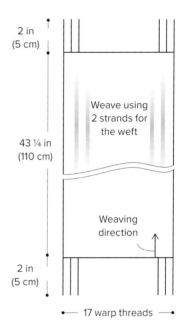

2 in
(5 cm)

Weave using
2 strands for
the weft

43 ¼ in
(110 cm)

Weaving
direction

2 in
(5 cm)

◄── 17 warp threads ──►

5. Use Method A on page 46 to create fringe using the warp threads.

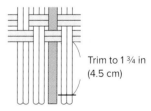

Trim to 1 ¾ in
(4.5 cm)

Tip: If using a single ply yarn, such as the Álafoss Lopi used in the sample, doubling it up in the warp and weft might result in the two adjacent yarn strands wanting to twist together. You may need to untwist the strands as you weave to produce a neat textile.

COLOR STUDY SCARF

Shown on page 21

FIBER

Use DK mohair/nylon blend yarn in the following colors:

Warp
- 25 yds (23 m) in blue
- 25 yds (23 m) in red
- 49 yds (45 m) in light green

Weft
- 73 yds (67 m) in variegated yellow

FINISHED PROJECT SIZE

7 x 53 ¼ in (18 x 135 cm) including fringe

LOOM USED

Table loom: 8 ¾ in (22 cm) or wider

INSTRUCTIONS

1. Make a table loom, as shown on page 40. Refer to the strung length listed below when positioning the loom.

2. String the loom according to the specifications listed below. Follow the warp scheme shown below:

Number of Warp Threads: 22 (2 strands each)
Strung Width: 8 in (20 cm)
Strung Length: 55 in (140 cm)

Warp Color Scheme

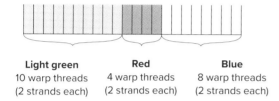

Light green	**Red**	**Blue**
10 warp threads	4 warp threads	8 warp threads
(2 strands each)	(2 strands each)	(2 strands each)

3. Insert a 2 ¾ in (7 cm) wide header to mark the fringe placement along the bottom of the loom, as shown on page 42.

4. Using two strands of weft thread, weave loosely for 49 ¾ in (126 cm). You should have about three rows every ¾ in (2 cm). Refer to page 43 for table loom weaving instructions.

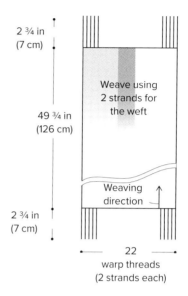

2 ¾ in (7 cm)

Weave using 2 strands for the weft

49 ¾ in (126 cm)

Weaving direction

2 ¾ in (7 cm)

22 warp threads (2 strands each)

5. Use Method A on page 46 to create fringe using the warp threads.

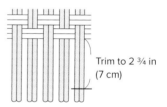

Trim to 2 ¾ in (7 cm)

LOOP SCARF

Shown on page 22

FIBER

Warp
- 39 yds (37 m) of super bulky alpaca yarn in brown

Both Warp & Weft
- 60 yds (55 m) of bulky wool/alpaca loop yarn in brown

OTHER MATERIALS

- Four ⅝ in (1.5 cm) diameter buttons
- Sewing thread

FINISHED PROJECT SIZE

6 ¼ x 45 ¼ in (16 x 115 cm) including fringe

LOOM USED

Table loom: 7 in (18 cm) or wider

INSTRUCTIONS

1. Make a table loom, as shown on page 40. Refer to the strung length listed below when positioning the loom.

2. String the loom according to the specifications listed below. Follow the warp color scheme shown on page 97, stringing the super bulky alpaca yarn first, then the bulky wool/alpaca loop yarn. Once the loom is strung, wind each warp thread tail around a nearby warp thread.

> **Number of Warp Threads:** 18 (2 strands each)
> **Strung Width:** 6 ¾ in (17 cm)
> **Strung Length:** 51 ¼ in (130 cm)

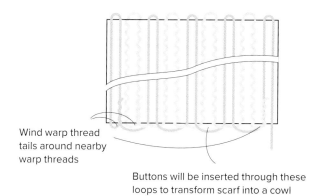

Wind warp thread tails around nearby warp threads

Buttons will be inserted through these loops to transform scarf into a cowl

Warp Color Scheme

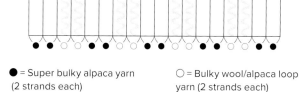

● = Super bulky alpaca yarn (2 strands each)

○ = Bulky wool/alpaca loop yarn (2 strands each)

3. Using one strand of weft thread, weave for 51 ¼ in (130 cm) using the no fringe Method C on page 47 (refer to page 43 for table loom weaving instructions).

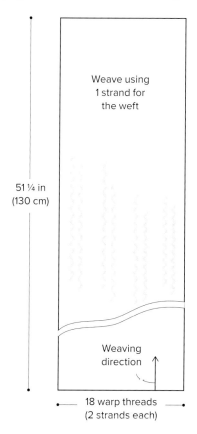

Weave using 1 strand for the weft

51 ¼ in (130 cm)

Weaving direction

18 warp threads (2 strands each)

4. Sew four buttons to the end of the scarf.

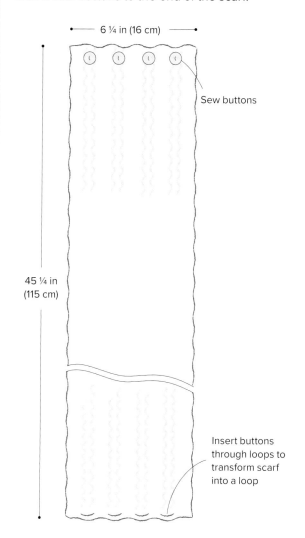

6 ¼ in (16 cm)

Sew buttons

45 ¼ in (115 cm)

Insert buttons through loops to transform scarf into a loop

Tip: Leave longer weft thread tails than normal at the beginning and end of weaving. If the wavy edges do not look right when you remove the scarf from the loom, you can weave the tails through to adjust the shape.

ARTIST'S MUFFLER

Shown on page 23

FIBER

Both Warp & Weft
- 54 yds (50 m) of super bulky slub wool yarn in multicolor

Warp
- 46 yds (42 m) of aran slub novelty yarn in blue

Weft
- 46 yds (42 m) of aran slub novelty yarn in mustard

FINISHED PROJECT SIZE

Width: 9 ½ in (24 cm)
Circumference: 28 ¼ in (72 cm)

LOOM USED

Box loom: At least 10 ¾ in (27 cm) wide with a 28 ¾ in (73 cm) circumference

INSTRUCTIONS

1. Locate a box matching the size requirements listed on page 98 or make your own box loom, as shown on page 59.

2. String the loom according to the specifications listed below.

> **Number of Warp Threads:** 22 (3 strands each: 2 strands of super bulky slub wool yarn + 1 strand of aran slub novelty yarn in blue)
> **Strung Width:** 9 ¾ in (25 cm)
> **Strung Circumference:** 28 ¾ in (73 cm)

3. Using three strands for the weft (2 strands of super bulky slub wool yarn + 1 strand of aran slub novelty yarn in mustard), weave around the circumference of the box, as shown on page 60.

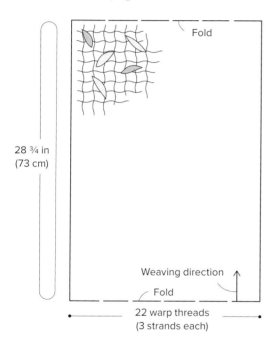

28 ¾ in (73 cm)

Fold

Weaving direction

Fold

22 warp threads (3 strands each)

Warp: 3 strands (2 strands of super bulky slub wool yarn + 1 strand of aran slub novelty yarn in blue)

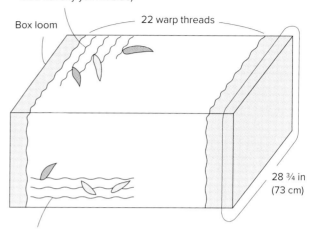

Box loom

22 warp threads

28 ¾ in (73 cm)

Weft: 3 strands (2 strands of super bulky slub wool yarn + 1 strand of aran slub novelty yarn in mustard)

4. Finish the thread tails, as shown on page 61.

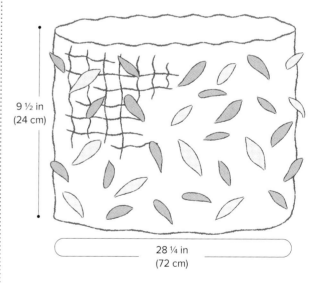

9 ½ in (24 cm)

28 ¼ in (72 cm)

GRASSY MEADOW WRAP

Shown on page 24

FIBER

Warp

- 44 yds (40 m) of DK mohair loop yarn in khaki
- 79 yds (72 m) of DK cotton/nylon loop yarn in light green
- 50 yds (45 m) of fingering ribbon novelty yarn in green
- 33 yds (30 m) of bulky furry novelty yarn in green

Weft

- 88 yds (80 m) of bulky pom-pom novelty yarn in green
- 66 yds (60 m) of bulky mohair/wool loop yarn in light green

FINISHED PROJECT SIZE

15 ½ x 59 in (39 x 150 cm) including fringe

LOOM USED

Table loom: 17 ¾ in (45 cm) or wider

Tip: If you cannot find a piece of cardboard wide enough to make the loom, use two pieces aligned side by side. If your table is not long enough to hold the loom, set it up on the floor.

INSTRUCTIONS

1. Make a table loom, as shown on page 40. Refer to the strung length listed below when positioning the loom.

2. String the loom according to the specifications listed below. Follow the warp color scheme shown below.

> **Number of Warp Threads:** 49 (2 strands of fingering ribbon novelty yarn, 1 strand of all other yarns)
> **Strung Width:** 16 ¼ in (41 cm)
> **Strung Length:** 59 in (150 cm)

Warp Color Scheme

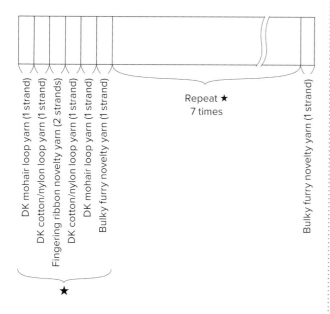

Repeat ★
7 times

DK mohair loop yarn (1 strand)
DK cotton/nylon loop yarn (1 strand)
Fingering ribbon novelty yarn (2 strands)
DK cotton/nylon loop yarn (1 strand)
DK mohair loop yarn (1 strand)
Bulky furry novelty yarn (1 strand)
Bulky furry novelty yarn (1 strand)

★

3. Insert a 2 ¾ in (7 cm) wide header to mark the fringe placement along the bottom of the loom, as shown on page 42.

4. Using the weft thread noted in the diagram, weave loosely for 55 ½ in (141 cm). You should have about three rows every ¾ in (2 cm). Refer to page 43 for table loom weaving instructions.

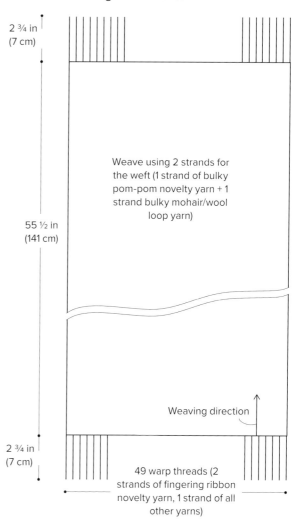

2 ¾ in (7 cm)

55 ½ in (141 cm)

Weave using 2 strands for the weft (1 strand of bulky pom-pom novelty yarn + 1 strand bulky mohair/wool loop yarn)

Weaving direction

2 ¾ in (7 cm)

49 warp threads (2 strands of fingering ribbon novelty yarn, 1 strand of all other yarns)

5. Use Method A on page 46 to create fringe using the warp threads.

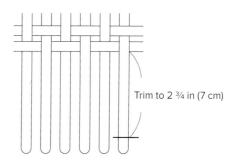

Trim to 2 ¾ in (7 cm)

SNOWFLAKE SHAWL

Shown on page 25

FIBER

Warp

- 16 yds (14 m) of super bulky wool twisted roving yarn in white
- 73 yds (66 m) of DK mohair/nylon yarn in white
- 27 yds (24 m) of bulky mohair/wool loop novelty yarn in white
- 88 yds (80 m) of fingering mohair/nylon loop novelty yarn in white

Warp & Weft

- 105 yds (96 m) of bulky wool/nylon loop novelty yarn in white

FINISHED PROJECT SIZE

16 ¼ x 59 in (41 x 150 cm) including fringe

LOOM USED

Table loom: 17 ¾ in (45 cm) or wider

Warp Color Scheme

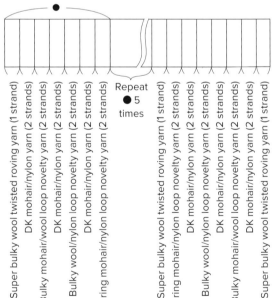

Super bulky wool twisted roving yarn (1 strand)
DK mohair/nylon yarn (2 strands)
Bulky mohair/wool loop novelty yarn (2 strands)
DK mohair/nylon yarn (2 strands)
Bulky wool/nylon loop novelty yarn (2 strands)
DK mohair/nylon yarn (2 strands)
Fingering mohair/nylon loop novelty yarn (2 strands)

Repeat
● 5 times

Super bulky wool twisted roving yarn (1 strand)
Fingering mohair/nylon loop novelty yarn (2 strands)
DK mohair/nylon yarn (2 strands)
Bulky wool/nylon loop novelty yarn (2 strands)
DK mohair/nylon yarn (2 strands)
Bulky mohair/wool loop novelty yarn (2 strands)
DK mohair/nylon yarn (2 strands)
Super bulky wool twisted roving yarn (1 strand)

INSTRUCTIONS

1. Make a table loom, as shown on page 40. Refer to the strung length listed below when positioning the loom.

2. String the loom according to the specifications listed below and the warp color scheme on the right.

Number of Warp Threads: 50 (1 strand of super bulky wool twisted roving yarn, 2 strands of all other yarns)
Strung Width: 17 ¼ in (44 cm)
Strung Length: 61 in (155 cm)

3. Insert a 2 ¾ in (7 cm) wide header to mark the fringe placement along the bottom of the loom, as shown on page 42.

4. Using one strand of weft thread, weave loosely for 55 ½ in (141 cm). You should have about three rows every ¾ in (2 cm). Refer to page 43 for table loom weaving instructions.

5. Use Method A on page 46 to create fringe using the warp threads.

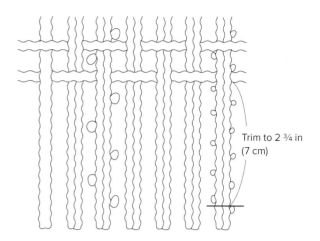

Trim to 2 ¾ in (7 cm)

Tip: If you cannot find a piece of cardboard wide enough to make the loom, use two pieces aligned side by side. If your table is not long enough to hold the loom, set it up on the floor.

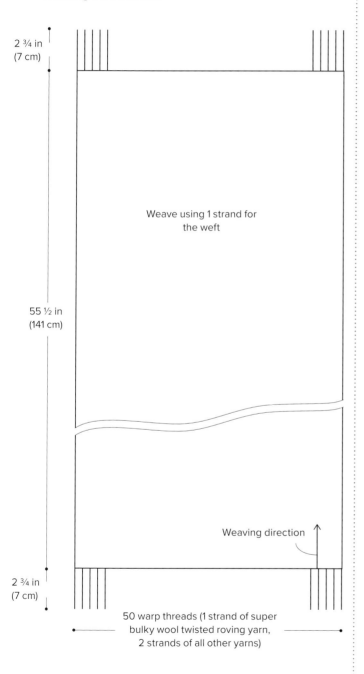

2 ¾ in (7 cm)

Weave using 1 strand for the weft

55 ½ in (141 cm)

Weaving direction

2 ¾ in (7 cm)

50 warp threads (1 strand of super bulky wool twisted roving yarn, 2 strands of all other yarns)

FLUFFY WRIST WARMERS

Shown on page 26

FIBER

Both Warp & Weft
- 66 yds (61 m) of bulky furry novelty yarn in brown

FINISHED PROJECT SIZE

Length: 7 ½ in (19 cm)
Outside Circumference: 10 ¼ in (26 cm)

LOOM USED

Box loom: At least 9 ½ in (24 cm) wide with a 9 in (23 cm) circumference

INSTRUCTIONS

1. Locate a box matching the size requirements listed on page 104 or make your own box loom, as shown on page 59.

2. String the loom according to the specifications listed below.

> **Number of Warp Threads:** 20 (2 strands each)
> **Strung Width:** 8 ¼ in (21 cm)
> **Strung Circumference:** 9 in (23 cm)

3. Using one strand for the weft, weave loosely around the circumference of the box, leaving a ⅜ in (1 cm) gap between rows. Refer to page 60 for box loom weaving instructions.

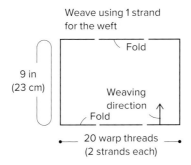

Weave using 1 strand for the weft
Fold
9 in (23 cm)
Weaving direction
Fold
20 warp threads (2 strands each)

4. Finish the thread tails, as shown on page 61.

5. Repeat steps 2-4 to make a second wrist warmer.

6. Insert your hands into the wrist warmers. Make the thumb holes by inserting your thumbs into the gap between two rows.

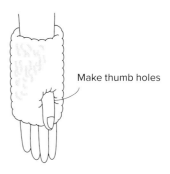

Make thumb holes

Finished Diagram

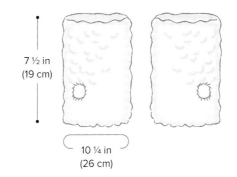

7 ½ in (19 cm)

10 ¼ in (26 cm)

COLORFUL WRIST WARMERS

Shown on page 26

FIBER

Warp
- 31 yds (28 m) of DK cotton yarn in cream

Both Warp & Weft
- 70 yds (64 m) of DK cotton ribbon novelty yarn in multicolor orange
- 27 yds (24 m) of DK cotton/nylon loop novelty yarn in cream

FINISHED PROJECT SIZE

Length: 8 in (20 cm)
Outside Circumference: 8 ¾ in (22 cm)

LOOM USED

Box loom: At least 9 ½ in (24 cm) wide with a 9 in (23 cm) circumference

INSTRUCTIONS

1. Locate a box matching the size requirements listed on page 106 or make your own box loom, as shown on page 59.

2. String the loom according to the specifications listed below. Follow the warp color scheme shown below. The DK cotton/nylon loop novelty yarn is used only for the first and last warp threads.

> **Number of Warp Threads:** 27 (see diagram below)
> **Strung Width:** 8 ¼ in (21 cm)
> **Strung Circumference:** 9 in (23 cm)

Warp Color Scheme

DK cotton/nylon loop novelty yarn (2 strands)

DK cotton yarn (1 strand) + DK cotton ribbon novelty yarn (2 strands)

Repeat ● 24 more times

DK cotton/nylon loop novelty yarn (2 strands)

3 strands = ●

3. Using three strands for the weft (2 strands of DK cotton ribbon novelty yarn + 1 strand of DK cotton/nylon loop novelty yarn), weave loosely around the circumference of the box, as shown on page 60. You should have about two rows every ⅜ in (1 cm).

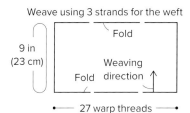

Weave using 3 strands for the weft

9 in (23 cm)

Fold

Fold

Weaving direction

27 warp threads

4. Finish the thread tails, as shown on page 61.

5. Repeat steps 2-4 to make a second wrist warmer.

6. Insert your hands into the wrist warmers. Make the thumb holes by inserting your thumbs between strands of yarn, about 8 rows from the end.

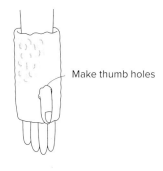

Make thumb holes

7. Use one strand of DK cotton/nylon loop novelty yarn to buttonhole stitch around the thumb holes.

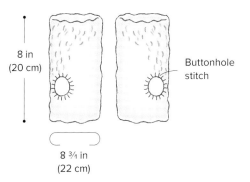

8 in (20 cm)

Buttonhole stitch

8 ¾ in (22 cm)

LOVELY LEG WARMERS

Shown on page 27

FIBER

Both Warp & Weft
- 131 yds (121 m) of aran furry novelty yarn in red

Weft
- 33 yds (31 m) of aran furry novelty yarn in brown

FINISHED PROJECT SIZE

Length: 9 ½ in (24 cm)
Outside Circumference: 13 ¾ in (35 cm)

LOOM USED

Box loom: At least 11 in (28 cm) wide with a 14 ½ in (37 cm) circumference

INSTRUCTIONS

1. Locate a box matching the size requirements listed above or make your own box loom, as shown on page 59.

2. String the loom according to the specifications listed below.

> **Number of Warp Threads:** 24 (2 strands each)
> **Strung Width:** 10 ¼ in (26 cm)
> **Strung Circumference:** 14 ½ in (37 cm)

3. Using two strands of red yarn for the weft, start weaving loosely around the circumference of the box, as shown on page 60. You should have about two rows every ⅜ in (1 cm).

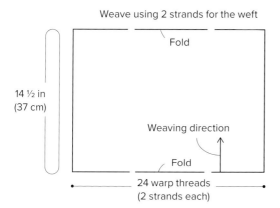

Weave using 2 strands for the weft

Fold

14 ½ in (37 cm)

Weaving direction

Fold

24 warp threads (2 strands each)

4. Change to the brown yarn to weave the desired stripe pattern, then continue weaving with the red yarn.

Stripe Pattern Diagrams

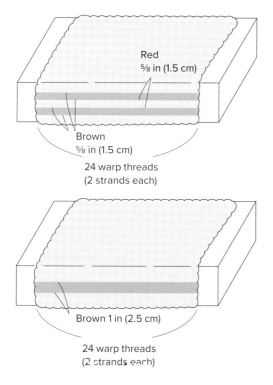

Red ⅝ in (1.5 cm)

Brown ⅝ in (1.5 cm)

24 warp threads (2 strands each)

Brown 1 in (2.5 cm)

24 warp threads (2 strands each)

5. Finish the thread tails, as shown on page 61.

6. Repeat steps 2-5 to make a second leg warmer.

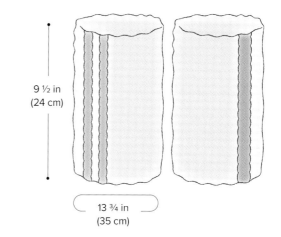

9 ½ in (24 cm)

13 ¾ in (35 cm)

If you find your leg warmers sliding down when you wear them, try sewing elastic around the top to create a better fit.

BUTTON CAP

Shown on page 28

FIBER

Both Warp & Weft
- 48 yds (44 m) of bulky alpaca plied yarn in beige
- 40 yds (47 m) of bulky alpaca plied yarn in light brown

Weft
- 22 yds (21 m) of aran furry novelty yarn in ivory

OTHER MATERIALS

- Two ⅜ in (1 cm) diameter felt pom-poms in beige

FINISHED PROJECT SIZE

Depth: 8 ¾ in (22 cm)
Head Circumference: 22 ½-22 ¾ in (57-58 cm)

LOOM USED

Box loom: At least 9 ½ in (24 cm) wide with a 23 ¼ in (59 cm) circumference

INSTRUCTIONS

1. Locate a box matching the size requirements listed above or make your own box loom, as shown on page 59.

2. String the loom according to the specifications listed at right. Follow the layout shown at right, leaving long tails on the beige yarn. These will eventually become the bow.

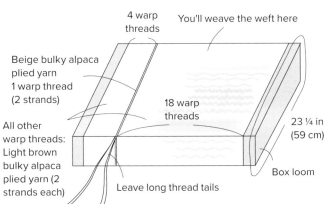

4 warp threads

You'll weave the weft here

Beige bulky alpaca plied yarn 1 warp thread (2 strands)

18 warp threads

23 ¼ in (59 cm)

All other warp threads: Light brown bulky alpaca plied yarn (2 strands each)

Leave long thread tails

Box loom

Number of Warp Threads: 23 (2 strands each)
Strung Width: 9 in (23 cm)
Strung Circumference: 23 ¼ in (59 cm)

3. Using two strands for the weft, weave around the circumference of the box, following the weft color scheme shown below. Refer to page 60 for box loom weaving instructions.

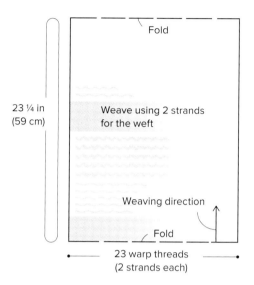

Fold

23 ¼ in
(59 cm)

Weave using 2 strands
for the weft

Weaving direction

Fold

23 warp threads
(2 strands each)

Weft Color Scheme

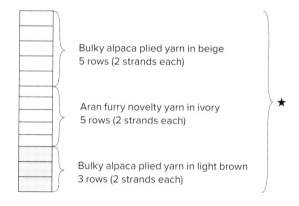

Bulky alpaca plied yarn in beige
5 rows (2 strands each)

Aran furry novelty yarn in ivory
5 rows (2 strands each)

★

Bulky alpaca plied yarn in light brown
3 rows (2 strands each)

Repeat ★ pattern around circumference of box, ending with bulky alpaca plied yarn in light brown. You may need to weave an additional row of light brown for the last repeat in order to complete the loop around the box.

4. Finish the weft thread tails as shown on page 61 and remove the textile from the loom. Finish one of the light brown warp thread tails, as shown on page 61.

5. Tie the beige warp thread tails in a bow, trim the excess yarn, and knot the ends. Use the remaining light brown warp thread tail to whipstitch the top of the hat closed. Sew the felt pom-poms to the two top corners of the hat using bulky alpaca plied yarn in light brown. Tie the yarn into a loop and trim the excess. Use the loops and pom-poms to fasten the hat.

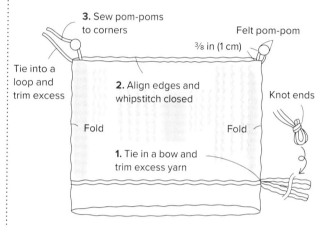

3. Sew pom-poms
to corners

Felt pom-pom

⅜ in (1 cm)

Tie into a
loop and
trim excess

2. Align edges and
whipstitch closed

Knot ends

Fold

Fold

1. Tie in a bow and
trim excess yarn

Finished Diagram

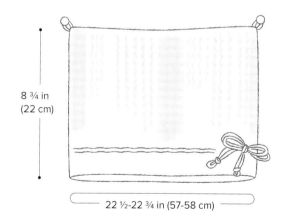

8 ¾ in
(22 cm)

22 ½-22 ¾ in (57-58 cm)

POM-POM HAT

Shown on page 29

FIBER

Warp
- 32 yds (30 m) of super bulky wool yarn in turquoise

Weft
- 35 yds (32 m) of super bulky wool yarn in variegated white/pink

FINISHED PROJECT SIZE

Depth: 8 ¼ in (21 cm)
Head Circumference: 22 ¾ in (58 cm)

LOOM USED

Box loom: At least 9 ½ in (24 cm) wide with a 23 ¼ in (59 cm) circumference

INSTRUCTIONS

1. Locate a box matching the size requirements listed on page 112 or make your own box loom, as shown on page 59.

2. String the loom according to the specifications listed below:

> **Number of Warp Threads:** 20 (2 strands each)
> **Strung Width:** 8 ¾ in (22 cm)
> **Strung Circumference:** 23 ¼ in (59 cm)

3. Using two strands for the weft, weave around the circumference of the box, as shown on page 60.

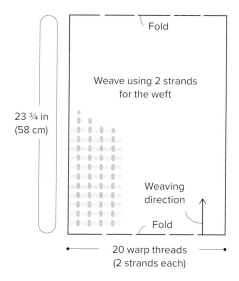

23 ¾ in (58 cm)

Fold

Weave using 2 strands for the weft

Weaving direction

Fold

20 warp threads (2 strands each)

4. Finish the weft thread tails as shown on page 61 and remove the textile from the loom. Finish one of the warp thread tails, as shown on page 61.

5. Pull the remaining warp thread tail to gather the textile into a hat shape and sew closed, as shown on page 62.

6. Make a pom-pom and sew to the top of the hat.

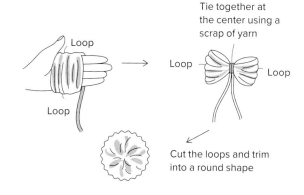

Wrap one strand of each color yarn around your hand 40 times total

Loop

Loop

Tie together at the center using a scrap of yarn

Loop

Loop

Cut the loops and trim into a round shape

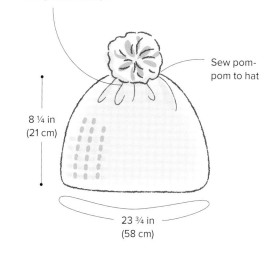

This end of the hat was gathered together in step 5

8 ¼ in (21 cm)

Sew pom-pom to hat

23 ¾ in (58 cm)

TOTE & DRAWSTRING POUCH SET

Shown on page 30

FOR THE TOTE

FIBER

Warp
- 21 yds (20 m) of super bulky acrylic roving in navy

Weft
- 21 yds (20 m) of super bulky acrylic roving in purple

Both Warp & Weft
- 51 yds (41 m) of hemp cord in black

OTHER MATERIALS

- One set of 16 in (40 cm) long black leather handles
- 4 in (10 cm) square of black felt
- Black embroidery floss
- Craft glue

FINISHED PROJECT SIZE

13 ¾ x 9 in (35 x 23 cm) without handles

LOOM USED

Box loom: At least 11 ¾ in (30 cm) wide with a 28 ¾ in (73 cm) circumference

INSTRUCTIONS

1. Locate a box matching the size requirements listed on page 114 or make your own box loom, as shown on page 59.

2. String the loom according to the specifications listed below.

> **Number of Warp Threads:** 30 (2 strands each: 1 strand of super bulky acrylic roving in navy + 1 strand of hemp cord in black)
> **Strung Width:** 11 in (28 cm)
> **Strung Circumference:** 28 ¾ in (73 cm)

3. Using two strands for the weft, weave around the circumference of the box, as shown on page 60.

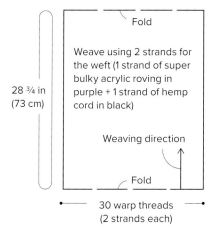

4. Finish the weft thread tails as shown on page 61 and remove the textile from the loom. Finish one of the warp thread tails, as shown on page 61.

5. Pull the remaining warp thread tail to gather the textile into a bag shape that is about 3 ⅛ in (8 cm) wide at the bottom, as shown on page 62. Use the warp thread tail to whipstitch the bag closed along the bottom. Turn the bag right side out.

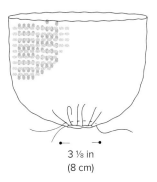

3 ⅛ in
(8 cm)

6. Sew the handles to the bag: Cut four pieces of felt matching the size and shape of the handle ends. Glue the handles to the outside of the bag following the placement noted below. Glue the felt supports to the inside of the bag. Use the embroidery floss to stitch the handles and felt supports in place.

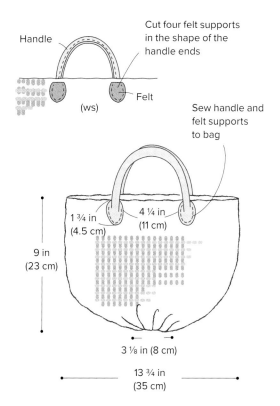

FOR THE DRAWSTRING POUCH

FIBER

Warp
- 9 yds (9 m) of super bulky acrylic roving in purple

Weft
- 5 yds (5 m) of super bulky acrylic roving in navy
- 15 yds (14 m) of hemp cord in black

OTHER MATERIALS

- Two 19 ¾ in (50 cm) long pieces of black leather cord

FINISHED PROJECT SIZE

5 x 7 in (12.5 x 18 cm)

LOOM USED

Flat loom for double-sided weaving:
8 in (20 cm) wide x 5 ½ in (14 cm) long

INSTRUCTIONS

1. Make a flat loom for double-sided weaving, as shown on page 53.

2. String the loom according to the specifications listed below.

> **Number of Warp Threads:** 22 (1 strand each)
> **Strung Width:** 7 ½ in (19 cm)
> **Strung Length:** 5 ½ in (14 cm)

3. Using two strands for the weft (1 strand of super bulky acrylic roving in navy + 1 strand of hemp cord in black), weave tightly for 11 in (28 cm), as shown on page 54.

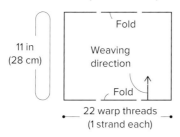

Weave using 2 strands for the weft (1 strand of super bulky acrylic roving in navy + 1 strand of hemp cord in black)

11 in (28 cm)

Fold

Weaving direction

Fold

22 warp threads (1 strand each)

4. Finish the thread tails and remove the textile from the loom.

5. Use a tapestry needle to insert one of the leather cords into the left side of the pouch. Weave over two weft stitches, then under two around the entire circumference of the pouch, ending where you began. Tie the two ends of the cord together. Repeat on the right side of the pouch to complete the drawstrings.

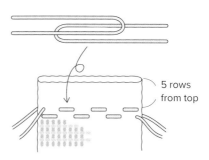

5 rows from top

Weave each piece of leather cord over and under two weft stitches

Finished Diagram

7 in (18 cm)

5 in (12.5 cm)

POM-POM SHOULDER BAG

Shown on page 31

FIBER

Warp
- 104 yds (95 m) of lace flag novelty yarn in rose
- 4 ¼ x 47 ¼ in (11 x 120 cm) of solid linen fabric

Weft
- 23 yds (21 m) of cotton/silk ladder novelty yarn in beige
- 175 yds (160 m) of bulky pom-pom yarn in red

OTHER MATERIALS

- Two 27 ½ in (70 cm) long pieces of 1 in (2.3 cm) wide linen ribbon
- 9 ¾ x 15 ¾ in (24.5 x 40 cm) of dark pink fabric for lining
- Sewing thread
- Craft glue

FINISHED PROJECT SIZE

7 ½ x 9 in (19 x 23 cm)

LOOM USED

Flat loom for double-sided weaving: 10 ¼ in (26 cm) wide x 8 in (20 cm) long

INSTRUCTIONS

1. Make a flat loom for double-sided weaving, as shown on page 53.

2. Cut the linen fabric into ½ in (1.2 cm) wide strips and glue together, as shown on page 58. These strips will be used as one of the warp threads.

3. String the loom according to the specifications listed below.

> **Number of Warp Threads:** 25 (2 strands each: 1 strand of lace flag novelty yarn + 1 strand of linen fabric)
> **Strung Width:** 9 ½ in (24 cm)
> **Strung Length:** 8 in (20 cm)

4. Using two strands for the weft (1 strand of cotton/silk ladder novelty yarn + 1 strand of bulky pom-pom yarn), weave for 8 in (20 cm), as shown on page 54.

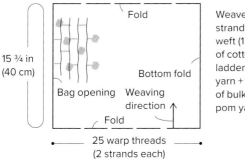

15 ¾ in (40 cm)

Fold

Bottom fold

Bag opening
Weaving direction ↑

Fold

Weave using 2 strands for the weft (1 strand of cotton/silk ladder novelty yarn + 1 strand of bulky pom-pom yarn)

25 warp threads (2 strands each)

5. Finish the thread tails and remove the textile from the loom.

6. Make the lining: Cut the fabric to the dimensions provided in the materials list. Fold the lining fabric in half with right sides together. Sew along the bottom and side using ⅜ in (1 cm) seam allowance.

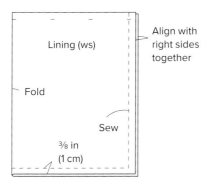

Lining (ws)

Align with right sides together

Fold

Sew

⅜ in (1 cm)

7. Fold the seams as shown and press with an iron. Along the bag opening, fold the seam allowance over ⅜ in (1 cm) to the wrong side and press.

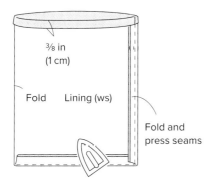

⅜ in (1 cm)

Fold   Lining (ws)

Fold and press seams

8. Use a toothpick to apply glue to the lace flag novelty yarn and adhere it to the pieces of linen ribbon. You'll want to glue the novelty yarn to both sides of the ribbon. Next, sew the two pieces of ribbon to the lining as shown.

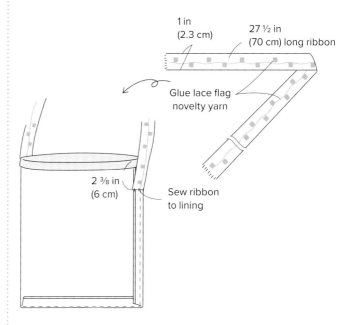

1 in (2.3 cm)

27 ½ in (70 cm) long ribbon

Glue lace flag novelty yarn

2 ⅜ in (6 cm)

Sew ribbon to lining

9. Insert the lining inside the textile. Pull the ribbon handles through the woven grain to the outside of the bag. Sew to outside of bag to secure. Hand stitch the lining to the textile around the bag opening.

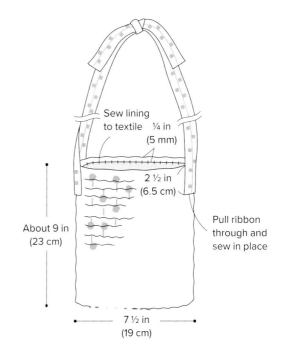

Sew lining to textile   ¼ in (5 mm)

2 ½ in (6.5 cm)

About 9 in (23 cm)

Pull ribbon through and sew in place

7 ½ in (19 cm)

CONFETTI CLUTCH

Shown on page 31

FIBER

Warp
- 26 yds (23 m) of DK pom-pom yarn in variegated blue/purple

Weft
- 4 ¾ x 43 ¼ in (12 x 110 cm) of blue cotton organdy fabric

OTHER MATERIALS

- One snap
- Sewing thread
- Craft glue

FINISHED PROJECT SIZE

5 ¼ x 4 in (13.5 x 10 cm)

LOOM USED

Flat loom for double-sided weaving with a flap: 5 ½ in (14 cm) wide x 11 in (28 cm) long

INSTRUCTIONS

1. Make a flat loom for double-sided weaving with a flap, as shown on page 123.

2. String the loom according to the specifications listed below. Also refer to page 56.

> **Number of Warp Threads:** 26 on front/25 on back (1 strand each)
> **Strung Width:** 5 ½ in (14 cm)
> **Strung Length:** 11 in (28 cm)

3. Cut the cotton organdy fabric into 1 ¼ in (3 cm) wide strips and glue together, as shown on page 58. These strips will be used as the weft thread.

4. Using the strips, weave on both sides of the loom for 4 in (10 cm), as shown on page 56.

5. Next, continue weaving on the front of the loom only for 3 ⅛ in (8 cm) to create the flap, as shown in step 5 on page 57.

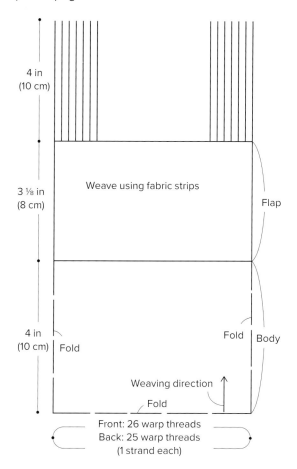

4 in
(10 cm)

3 ⅛ in
(8 cm)

Weave using fabric strips

Flap

4 in
(10 cm)

Fold

Fold

Fold

Body

Weaving direction

Fold

Front: 26 warp threads
Back: 25 warp threads
(1 strand each)

6. Cut the warp threads along the top of the loom, as shown in step 6 on page 57.

7. Finish the warp threads along the flap (refer to step 7 on page 57): Knot the warp threads together in sets of two to make fringe (one set will have three). If your yarn is fine, you may need to make a few knots, then apply some glue to secure. Trim the fringe to ¾ in (2 cm).

8. Finish the warp threads along the pouch opening (refer to step 8 on page 57): Knot the warp threads together in sets of two. Weave the warp threads in and trim the excess.

9. Sew one snap component to the pouch body and one snap component to the inside flap.

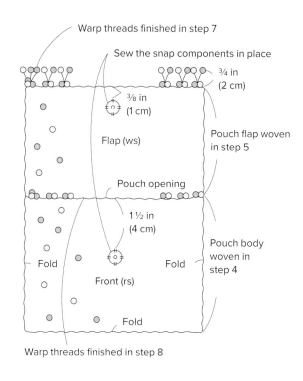

Warp threads finished in step 7

Sew the snap components in place

¾ in
(2 cm)

⅜ in
(1 cm)

Flap (ws)

Pouch flap woven
in step 5

Pouch opening

1 ½ in
(4 cm)

Fold

Fold

Front (rs)

Pouch body
woven in
step 4

Fold

Warp threads finished in step 8

Finished Diagram

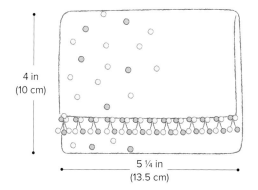

4 in
(10 cm)

5 ¼ in
(13.5 cm)

DESIGNING YOUR OWN PROJECTS

You'll find the required loom dimensions listed for each project in this book, but if you're interested in designing your own project, you'll need to determine the loom size for yourself. Use the following information to calculate the required loom size for projects woven on each type of cardboard loom.

TABLE LOOM (SEE PAGE 40)

When working on a table loom, it's important to note that you can weave textiles in a variety of widths, but that they will be ¾ in (2 cm) smaller than the width of the loom at maximum. If you are interested in weaving larger objects, just make a wider table loom.

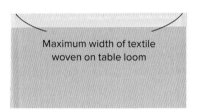

Maximum width of textile woven on table loom

FLAT LOOM (SEE PAGE 48)

Loom Width: Add 1 ½-2 in (4-5 cm) to the desired finished width of the textile.

Loom Length: The length of the loom should equal the desired finished length of the textile plus 4 in (10 cm) at each end for fringe (if desired). If you're planning to weave a textile longer than 8 in (20 cm), add an additional 1 ¼-2 in (3-5 cm) for shrinkage when removing the textile from the loom.

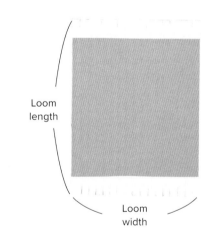

Loom length

Loom width

BOX LOOM (SEE PAGE 59)

Loom Width: Add 1 ¼ in (3 cm) to the desired finished width of the textile.

Loom Circumference: The circumference of the loom should equal the desired finished circumference of the textile, plus ⅜-⅝ in (1-1.5 cm) for shrinkage when removing the textile from the loom.

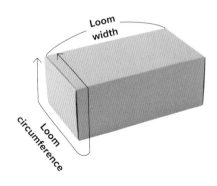

Loom width

Loom circumference

VARIATION: FLAT LOOM FOR ROUND TEXTILES (SEE PAGE 50)

To weave in the round, you'll need a square flat loom with notches cut into all four sides. Use the following formula to calculate the length to cut each of the four sides:

Desired diameter of your round woven textile +
Length of desired fringe (make sure to include both sides) +
Shrinkage when removing textile from loom

Note:

- When weaving a stretchy fiber, such as t-shirt yarn or jersey fabric, add an extra 1 ½-2 ½ in (4-6 cm) to accommodate for shrinkage when removing the textile from the loom.

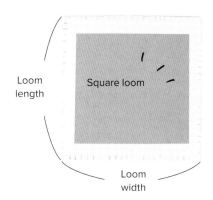

VARIATION: DOUBLE-SIDED WEAVING (SEE PAGE 53)

For this type of loom only, the loom length will dictate the width of the textile and the loom width will dictate the height of the textile.

Loom Width: Add 1 ¼ in (3 cm) or more to the desired finished height of the textile.

Loom Length: Add ⅜-⅝ in (1-1.5 cm) to the desired finished width of the textile. This will account for shrinkage when removing the textile from the loom.

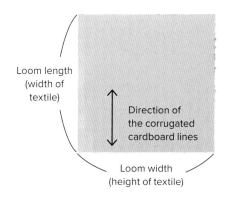

VARIATION: DOUBLE-SIDED WEAVING WITH A FLAP (SEE PAGE 56)

When working on this type of loom, it may help to use the items you wish to store in the pouch, such as credit cards or a cell phone, as a guide. Draw guidelines on the loom to mark the pouch opening and flap end.

Loom Width: Add ¾ in (2 cm) or more to the desired finished width of the pouch. This will form the side gussets of the pouch and create depth.

Loom Length: Use the following formula to calculate the loom length:

Pouch body = Desired finished height of the pouch + ⅝ in (1.5 cm)
or more (for the bottom gusset of the pouch) +
Length of the flap +
Length of the desired fringe (usually 3 ⅛-4 in [8-10 cm])

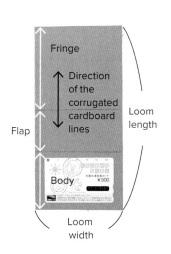

SHUTTLE

No need to buy a fancy wooden shuttle—you can make your own out of cardboard! Simply follow the instructions below to make a shuttle in no time.

CUTTING DIAGRAM

(not a template)

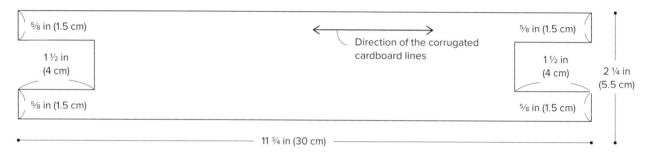

⅝ in (1.5 cm)

1 ½ in (4 cm)

⅝ in (1.5 cm)

Direction of the corrugated cardboard lines

⅝ in (1.5 cm)

1 ½ in (4 cm)

⅝ in (1.5 cm)

2 ¼ in (5.5 cm)

11 ¾ in (30 cm)

INSTRUCTIONS

1. Cut a 3 x 1 ⅞ in (8 x 4.5 cm) piece of fabric tape. Align the tape under one shuttle prong with the sticky side facing up.

2. Make ⅝ in (1.5 cm) long cuts at the center of the tape until you meet the cardboard shuttle.

3. Fold the top left and bottom left portions of the tape in to cover one prong.

4. Fold the right portion of tape in to cover the same prong as in step 3.

5. Fold the remaining sections of the tape down to cover the same prong a second time.

Repeat steps 1-5 to cover the remaining three shuttle prongs.

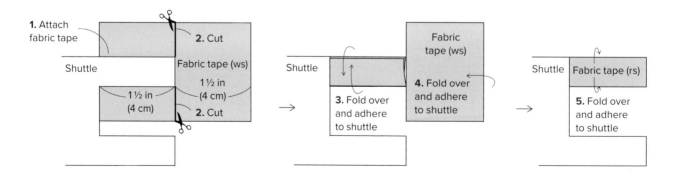

1. Attach fabric tape

Shuttle

2. Cut

Fabric tape (ws)

1 ½ in (4 cm)

1 ½ in (4 cm)

2. Cut

Shuttle

Fabric tape (ws)

3. Fold over and adhere to shuttle

4. Fold over and adhere to shuttle

Shuttle

Fabric tape (rs)

5. Fold over and adhere to shuttle

INDEX

HARUMI KAGEYAMA started her career in craft book publishing and became known for her "easy to make and easy to use" projects using natural and found materials like twigs, driftwood, wire, and fabric. She has contributed to handicraft segments on TV and radio and also teaches classes that focus on upcycling materials. She is the author of several books on weaving and crafting published in Japan. Her website is www.kageyamaharumi.com.